Be a Better
In A Week

Rus Slater

ned to any

Rus Slater began his career in the world of TV advertising before eventually joining the British Army. After initial basic training Rus went to the Royal Military Academy Sandhurst and was trained in 'man-management' and leadership, before going on to the Royal School of Military Engineering to learn specialist 'combat engineering' management.

For the following six years Rus galloped about the Western Hemisphere, managing and leading, teaching and learning. During this time he managed flood relief and dam repair in the UK, airfield construction and building in Central America, major exercises in northern Germany, and teaching in the UK and Bavaria. He was instrumental in managing an element of the 1987 Royal Tournament shortly before leaving the service.

Since returning to civilian life Rus has managed teams of employees as their formal reporting manager. He has managed and led volunteers working for nothing for charities. He has managed virtual teams of self-employed people executing commercial contracts. He has also managed to write six management books.

Be a Better Manager

Rus Slater

www.inaweek.co.uk

Teach® Yourself

Contents

Introduction

I was really lucky – very early in my career, even before I was actually given management responsibility, I was formally trained in management. It wasn't a week-long course; I spent six months at a residential centre. It wasn't all pure management; I also learned a lot of technical information and worked a lot on my stamina and physical fitness. Since then my stamina has increased with age, and my physical fitness has decreased for the same reason! But the foundation of management knowledge and skill remains with me and I have built on it over the years. It is this knowledge and experience that this book aims to distil into seven straightforward chapters.

Management, however, isn't a 'seven-day wonder'. There is no idiot-proof guide that will give you the answer for every situation. Good management is a blend of knowledge, skills and habits that you need to practise on a daily basis.

As you settle into your role of managing people, you will learn a great deal about human psychology, about communication, about yourself. You will learn that the best-laid plans will often not work and that sometimes you and your people will succeed owing to pure chance and good luck. Management is as much about giving luck a helping hand as it is about having all the answers.

When you manage people, you take on many different responsibilities:

- You take on responsibility **from your boss** – he or she is now entrusting you, and delegating to *you*, the authority and the accountability for achieving.
- You take on responsibility **to your customers**, be they internal or real, paying clients – they now trust you to make sure that they get what they want or are paying for.

- You take on responsibility **from your staff, team or people** – they now look to *you* to be the person with the answers, the person who will provide them with work and the person who will protect them.
- You take on responsibility **from your former boss** – you are now in the metaphorical driving seat; things that used to be done *for* you, you now have to do *for yourself*.

When you become a manager, you simply cannot continue to be the exact same person that you were when you didn't have all these extra responsibilities. You have to change. You have to think ahead – to the consequences of actions and the implications of decisions.

Stephen Covey wrote a book back in the 1980s (republished several times) entitled *The Seven Habits of Highly Effective People*. It has sold more than 25 million copies and is available in virtually every language. Covey defines 'effective' as including a high level of 'interdependence'. In this definition he explains that humans living in a society travel along a 'maturity continuum':

- As children, we are **dependent**. We depend on our parents, our guardians and our teachers. These people not only take responsibility for clothing, feeding and protecting us, but also for making our decisions for us.
- As we grow up, we develop **independence**. We take responsibility for ourselves; we look after ourselves and make our own decisions.
- When we are 'effective', we have developed **interdependence**. This means that we make decisions and take responsibility for being independent within a civil society, ensuring that our independence doesn't damage others. We work *with* people; we take mutually beneficial decisions.

To be a better manager you must develop your own interdependence.

SUNDAY

Understand your paradigm and get the job!

It is possible that you have bought this book in anticipation of a management role in the near future. You may be aiming to try to get appointed to a management position or you may currently be on a 'trial', with an 'acting rank'. If this is the case, then you will want to find ways of getting noticed and proving your ability to the people who make the decision and the people who influence the decision makers.

To reach your goal, you will have to understand your paradigm – or set of attitudes – regarding management:

- Do you see your management position as the reward for your previous technical competence? Or is it a totally new challenge that consists of a new set of tasks that you have yet to master?
- Does your appointment as a manager bring you kudos, power and the right to have others at your beck and call? Or does it bring responsibility, authority and a need to be more considerate of other people?
- Do you want to be loved as a manager? Or respected? Or do you want to be feared?

Today, then, we will look at two elements:

1 understanding what you want to be as a manager
2 getting the job, if you haven't actually been appointed yet.

Understand your paradigm...

In most careers, the only way to pay a person more money and give them higher status is to give them a 'higher' role and title. A person may become a 'senior' surveyor or a 'Leading' Seaman. Sometimes this can be done solely by giving them greater technical responsibility; they just manage process or machines, or they are simply given the responsibility to manage themselves with less supervision. For someone in this position they have no increased need to manage people; they have become more independent but no one is now dependent on them as a manager. However, in many industries, a person who is promoted becomes a team leader, a supervisor or a 'manager' of people immediately. This opens up a whole series of questions for the newly promoted person. Let's look at each of these in turn.

'Do I now have to leave all my old friends behind as I am now their boss and have to tell them what to do?'

To make the move from staff member to manager isn't a seismic shift; you are still part of the team. It is a small change of mental attitude; you are now a *different* part of the team. Now you have responsibilities and accountabilities that are different from your previous role, and different from those of your teammates.

If you remain too friendly *with specific members* of the team, you will create subgroups of favourites. This is detrimental to team spirit and you will soon find that your former workmates are fragmenting into little cliques who work in spite of each other rather than with each other. You must now treat all your people with the same fairness, regardless of how close you may have been to some of them before you were promoted.

'Can't I simply continue doing the old job exactly as before but with a new title?'

For some people the thought of taking on the non-technical elements of the new role – of no longer being what they originally set out to be – creates something of a problem. If you were a shop assistant, for example, and you are now being promoted to shop manager then you are going to spend:

- less time on the shop floor and more time in the back office
- less time with customers and more time counting stock in the stockroom
- less time operating the till and more time on doing spread sheets of sales and margins
- less time solving customers' problems and more time reporting monthly figures to head office.

This is a fundamental shift in your focus and a significant shift in your day-to-day activities, but you still connect to, and interact with, your former colleagues and your former role.

It is important to recognize these differences and to embrace them and make changes to your underlying attitude; if you don't, you run the risk of being ineffective as a manager.

The Peter Principle

There is a concept in management that is called the 'Peter Principle'. This suggests that most people are promoted to their level of incompetence. For instance:

- A person became a nurse because she liked helping people.
- She was good at it, and this was recognized by her bosses, so they promoted her to be a senior nurse. This worked well for her because it gave her more autonomy and responsibility with patients and she thrived in the role.
- Her abilities were again noted and she was promoted to become a ward nurse. Now she looked after not just a few patients but an entire ward. Again she thrived in the role, revelling in the authority and initiative she was able to exercise.
- Her abilities were again noted and she was promoted to become the matron of the entire department. Now she had several ward nurses reporting to her and she had no patients of her own to care for. She spent her time arranging work rosters and admissions, managing the drugs and dealing with the logistics of cleaning and feeding.

- She had been excellent in the care and management of patients, but she was simply not motivated to leave that behind and manage staff and processes and procedures and policies. Bed-sheets? Yes! Spread sheets? No! Owing to her lack of motivation, she was simply not at all good at managing the staff who now reported to her... she had been promoted to her level of incompetence.

If you have been promoted then you must recognize the changes in your day-to-day role and your responsibilities.

'Now that I'm the boss, is my life a bed of roses and easier than it used to be, or am I actually going to have to work harder now that I ever did before?'

Many people see promotion to a management role as the indicator that they have now achieved the status and reward they deserve. This leads them to take the view that RHIP – 'rank has its privileges'. Their promotion brings them a higher salary, better benefits and the deference that comes with the extra power they have over the people who report to them.

Up to a point, this is entirely understandable: if there are no tangible benefits of promotion, what is there to motivate anyone to seek it? This paradigm becomes potentially destructive, however, if the power corrupts and the new manager simply expects the people who report to them to do *all* the work, while they simply enjoy the benefits of the rank.

However, there is an alternative way of looking at the issue. Now that you have been promoted to a management role, you may take the view of *noblesse oblige*, which means that with rank comes responsibility. You have obligations to the people who report to you; these obligations are yours alone and cannot be delegated.

There are eight responsibilities that a person takes on as a manager that they didn't necessarily have as a staff member:

1 to state the overall aims and norms of the team
2 to create meaningful targets for individuals and the team as a whole

SUNDAY

MONDAY

TUESDAY

WEDNESDAY

THURSDAY

FRIDAY

SATURDAY

3 to formulate the plans for the team
4 to communicate within, and on behalf of, the team
5 to motivate the team, as a team, and on an individual basis
6 to evaluate the levels of success that the team, and individual team members, achieve
7 to facilitate improvements within the team's sphere of interest; these may be in the working conditions, processes and procedures or people's skills and abilities
8 to berate/congratulate the team and its members on their failures and successes.

You will notice that none of them is directly related to the role that you *used* to fulfil as a staff member – they are all *in addition* to the technical role that you may still be expected to fulfil!

'Now that I'm the boss do I have to instinctively know what to do all the time?'

You shouldn't expect yourself to have become infallible overnight. You may have been promoted because you are brighter and better than any of the people who work for you, but you are not omnipotent. Better managers have the confidence to know when they don't know, or when it is better to ask other people so they can make the best decision. Let us take a look at the different decision-making styles you can adopt and the advantages and disadvantages of each.

Autocratic decision making

There is a huge temptation for you to make decisions alone and in an apparently 'decisive' manner. This is the 'loneliness of command' and 'the buck stops here' approach. You don't seek advice or opinions from others. You make decisions personally.

Pros of an autocratic approach	Cons of an autocratic approach
• It *looks* decisive • It *looks* as if you are in control • It is generally quicker • It avoids an uncontrolled 'talking shop' • People know where they stand; you make the decisions	• You may not personally have all the information available • It doesn't allow for other people's opinions • You carry the sole responsibility if it turns out to be the *wrong* decision • Some people will disagree solely because they weren't consulted • If you don't make a decision, then nothing will get done, because people won't take the initiative

An autocratic approach may work well with people who are used to simply doing as they are told. It is also sometimes the best tool when time is very tight and a response is needed quickly.

Democratic decision making

If you want to get other people's input, whether it is their intellectual knowledge or their opinion, you can open decisions out to a democratic vote. You can do this **formally**, by actually getting everyone together and getting a 'show of hands', or you can do it **informally** by speaking to people one at a time and asking their response.

Pros of a democratic approach	Cons of a democratic approach
• It tends to create 'buy in' – in other words, support for your ideas • It gives people a sense of worth and self-respect to have their opinions taken into account • It spreads the responsibility for success or failure	• It can take a lot of time • It can look as if you are not in control • It is open to 'horse trading' – people give their support in return for a 'favour' • You cannot please all the people all the time

A democratic approach is useful when the matter in hand is not urgent. It is also appropriate for decisions that are more social than business oriented; for instance, if you were making a decision about a team dinner or an interdepartmental sports league.

Consultative decision making

This is a combination of autocratic and democratic; you consult people to get their input but then *you* alone make the decision. You can consult on a one-to-one basis or in a group.

Pros of a consultative approach	Cons of a consultative approach
• You get all the information • It gives people a sense of worth and self-respect to have their opinions sought • It gets you people's subjective opinions • It gets people's creative input • It focuses the responsibility for success or failure on you	• It can take a lot of time • It can look as if you are not in possession of information that you perhaps should have • It can give people the impression that they are part of the decision when in fact the decision is yours • It focuses the responsibility for success or failure on you

A consultative approach is useful for matters that are important but not terribly urgent. In order to avoid some of the cons, it is critical to make people aware that you are asking their opinions, not giving them voting rights.

Whichever approach you use the most important thing is to ensure that decisions get made. On Thursday, you will see that most unnecessary delays in processes are due to poor decision making.

'Now that I'm the boss do I have to have all the answers all the time?'

As the boss, people will bring you questions all the time. Many managers feel a self-generated pressure to have the answers... every time. Again, it is not likely that, simply because you have been promoted, you suddenly become omniscient. If you try to answer every question immediately, you will undoubtedly get some spectacularly wrong. However, you have to ensure that you don't start to show impatience with people bringing you questions:

> **'The day soldiers stop bringing you their problems is the day you have stopped leading them. They have either lost confidence that you can help them or concluded that you do not care.'**
>
> Colin Powell, *A Leadership Primer*, Lesson 2
> (http://nets.ucar.edu/nets/intro/staff/jcustard/
> jc-la2004/powell-leadership.pdf)

This is potentially dangerous for several reasons:

- If you don't actually know the answer, you may give the wrong one; this could make you look clueless in fairly short order or it could have wider-reaching consequences later on.
- You may not be the right person to answer the question, so if you answer it you may be stepping outside your area of authority or expertise.
- By giving an answer you satisfy the questioner's short-term need. This conditions them to come back for more. Soon you will find that they are dependent on you for quick answers to all their questions. This puts a greater strain on you and reduces their ability to think for themselves. We will look again at this on Wednesday.

Use the '4 Ds' approach to people's questions

1 Delay it.

'That is a good question; I'm glad you asked. Could you come back at x o'clock and then we can take 10 minutes for me to explain the answer?'

This is a good strategy for several reasons:

– If the answer is one that you should have at your fingertips, but you have forgotten, it allows you to remind yourself without losing face.

– By putting in the short delay you increase the likelihood that the team member will work out the answer themselves and you will shortly get a call to say, 'Don't worry about the x o'clock meeting; I've sorted it out.' This is good for your people's development.

– Your team learns that, although you welcome and will answer all their questions, you are not available to them at their convenience. This allows you to better manage your time and workflow.

2 Defer it.

'That is a good question; I'm glad you asked but I need to think about that/look up the answer. Could you come back at x o'clock?'

This is a good strategy for several reasons:

– It openly shows that you think about things.
– It allows you time to schedule thinking or research time.

– By telling the team member that you will give their question intellectual effort, you assure them of their worth.

3 Deflect it.

– *'That is a good question, I'm glad you asked. What do you think?'* Deflecting it back to the asker shows that you value their opinion and believe that they have the ability to find their own answers. It also encourages them to think and to see that you want them to think.

– *'That is a good question, I'm glad you asked. I'd like you to go and look up the answer and then brief everyone at the team meeting on Tuesday.'* Deflecting it into a new task for the asker shows confidence in their abilities to develop independence. Giving them the secondary responsibility (to present their findings) shows that you have confidence in them and is also developmental.

– *'That is a good question; I'm glad you asked. Pat is the best person to give you an answer to that. Can you go and ask her?'* Deflecting it to the correct person (whether because it is a matter of authority; it is Pat's job or expertise; or Pat is simply the most likely to know) shows that you have the confidence in the correct person, know the reporting lines in the organization, and trust the team member to seek out the correct person and verbalize the question effectively to them.

4 **Deal with it.**

– *'That is a good question; I'm glad you asked. What you need to do is...'* When the answer is simple and quick and you can save time, for both you and the team member then just give them the answer.

'Now that I'm the boss I have to make sure that, whether people love me or hate me, they *fear* me'

When Niccolò Machiavelli wrote the book *The Prince* in the sixteenth century, he advised that a leader should rely most on people fearing him in order to ensure that they pay attention to him. That was probably quite good advice in a society where life was 'nasty, brutish and short', where law was almost non-existent and everyone was born into their place in the world. In the 21st century, however, it is more regularly accepted that, as a manager, you don't need to rule by fear and that in fact fear can be a very poor foundation for effective management.

In the English language there is the idiom 'When the cat's away, the mice will play'. For a manager this means that if your people (the mice) live in fear of you (the cat), then, when your back is turned (you are away), they will play (i.e. do no work). Certainly, you will find that if you have to intimidate people into working for you then you will have to check on them all the time. This means that you cannot take time off, you cannot be away from the workplace on business and, if you are in a separate office, they will slack at every opportunity.

However, if you win their 'hearts and minds' they will work for you with integrity and respect even when they know that you aren't there.

> ### 'Real integrity is doing the right thing, knowing that nobody's going to know whether you did it or not.'
>
> Oprah Winfrey

Winning the hearts and minds of your team requires you to demonstrate several different characteristics:

Let's look at each of these in turn.

Fairness

You need to treat your people with total fairness. This is not the same as treating everyone equally: there is nothing as unfair as treating unequal things equally.

Dos	Don'ts
• Recognize and reward effort and success • Recognize and manage poor performance • Be considerate to people's out-of-work lives	• Have favourites • Bear grudges or keep reminding people of past failures

Consistency

Your team must be able to develop a strong idea of what to expect from you in terms of your approach and behaviour.

Dos	Don'ts
• Think before you react to a situation • Try to plan contingency actions for changes • Explain your reasons for taking a particular course of action or decision	• Ask someone's opinion and then tell them not to argue with you • Tell someone to do as they are told and then ask them why they didn't think through the consequences of their actions

Integrity

You need to be able to place trust in your people; after all, they hold the key to the success or failure of your career. In order for you to be able to trust them, you need to let them see that they can trust you.

Dos	Don'ts
• Be scrupulously honest • Give trust where it is deserved • Lead by example • Be clear about the parameters of acceptable and unacceptable behaviour	• Turn a blind eye to dishonesty • Allow established practices of dishonesty to continue • Allow certain people to get away with things that others get censured for • Take credit for someone else's idea or success

Support

As the manager, you have to provide the people with the support they need to be able to do their jobs. This means different things for different people in different situations.

Dos	Don'ts
• Help people to achieve • Create a culture where asking for support is acceptable • Give the right type of support • Encourage people to support each other • Give people the benefit of the doubt in the event of a complaint; listen to all the evidence from both sides before judging	• Do it for them • Belittle a request for support • Assume that support is only needed when someone is failing • Assume that support is the solution to all problems

Challenge

People work best when they have a challenge to which they can rise. This includes you!

Dos	Don'ts
• Encourage people to welcome challenges, even to set their own • Give people a challenge that stretches them • Challenge yourself as well • Use challenges to improve people's skills and knowledge as well as to achieve goals • Give praise for challenges met • Encourage learning from the success and failure of challenges	• Let people fall into bad habits • Set people up to fail by setting too stretching challenges • Just try to squeeze more out of people by constantly moving targets higher • Criticize someone's use of initiative

...And get the job

If you are presently awaiting the opportunity to win promotion, you shouldn't simply sit and wait. While the meek may well inherit the earth, they may have to wait an inordinately long time before they get their hands on their just desserts. You may be lucky but:

> **Luck = opportunity + preparedness**

You have already begun to prepare; you have bought this book!

Now start to create some opportunities. Here are 10 top tips to gain a promotion:

1 **Go and ask for one.** You can apply for any promotion positions that become available and get advertised within the organization, whether they are directly in line with your current role or not. If there is nothing being advertised, then have a formal discussion with your boss and let him/her know that you actively want a promotion. If asked why, avoid mentioning such selfish-sounding reasons as 'I need/want more money', and instead talk about your abilities, skills and knowledge and how they could be of greater value to the organization in a managerial position. If there are no opportunities with your current employer, you need to seriously consider moving.

2 **Seek extra responsibility.** Identify extra responsibilities that you could take on that either:
   - add new value to your boss's standing, such as bringing a new element into the department, *or*
   - take some work off your boss by allowing him/her to delegate some of their work to you.

3 **Show initiative.** This can be done in any number of ways:
   - Propose a new product or service.
   - Propose an improvement to an existing in-house process.
   - Identify a new area of potential customers.
   - Identify a new route to market for the organization's products or services.

- Identify a new threat or risk to the organization.
- Solve a problem, particularly something that had the potential to escalate into something costly.
- Identify a potential new recruit.

Obviously, in order to make a full-scale business proposition out of your initial idea, you need to do the research and look at the savings, cost/benefit or expected return on investment.

4 **Think positively.** It is vital that you think positively about the situation that the organization is in and the position of the department in which you work. Negative people don't make good managers and sensible optimism (rather than just mindless enthusiasm) strengthens the chances of success. Always look on the bright side of everything and try to see the opportunity in every change in circumstance.

5 **Speak positively.** Don't *actively* criticize your colleagues, your boss, your organization, your products, your services or your customers. If you find yourself in a meeting (at work) or a bull-session (outside work) where this sort of talk occurs, actively try to turn the conversation around.

6 **Behave like a manager:**
- Dress like a manager, even on dress-down days – this includes all aspects of grooming.
- Think like a manager – start looking at the 'bigger-picture', consider the cost/benefit of different courses of action, ask why certain things are done in certain ways (this isn't the same as *questioning* your boss – it is about understanding *how* things work).
- Go the extra mile – most staff members get paid overtime if they work late; managers are expected to fulfil their role without watching the clock.
- Use your initiative – that is what managers are paid to do.

7 **Network like crazy.** When an opportunity comes up you want the decision makers to have your name close to the tip of their tongue. Take any and all opportunities to meet with these decision makers; this could be by actively making improvement suggestions mentioned in tip number 3 above, or it could be by contriving to meet them in the lift or meeting them at the water-cooler/coffee machine. If you

can't reach them directly, at least make your name known *positively* among their team members/departments.

8 **Create a job for yourself.** It is not unknown for people who are successful at tip 3 above to be able to create a whole new job for themselves.

Case study

Steve was a junior in the marketing department when he saw an opportunity for the company to both reduce its energy bills and gain valuable environmental PR. He investigated the possibilities and approached his boss with a well-thought-out proposition. He persisted and eventually got the go-ahead to get some professional advice. He asked if he could manage this, and was given the job. Then, on the back of that, he was authorized to run a limited pilot programme. When that was successful, he was formally appointed to a newly created management position to take the programme nationwide.

9 **Do your current job really well.** Suffice to say, failing (or even being average) in your current role, is not a likely springboard to career success! Master your current role and teach others how to do it well. This latter point is critical – your boss will be reluctant to promote you if, in doing so, they will simply be losing a good worker. By making sure that you have a successor, you are freeing yourself up to be promoted.

10 **Make sure people know how good you are.** Although you don't want to appear arrogant, if you are so meek that you are invisible you will simply be passed over. If you achieve something, be proud of it. You could:
   – write an article for the company newsletter
   – tweet or blog about it (being careful not to break any commercial confidences)
   – offer to talk about it at the next team or department meeting
   – publicize it in any appropriate trade or professional magazines or websites.

Summary

On Sunday you have looked at understanding your fundamental attitude to becoming a manager. If you get this attitude 'right', you will be able to be consistent in your dealings with your team. It will improve your confidence, and this in turn will give your team confidence as well. It will allow you to trust them and they you. In short, it will make you a better manager.

You have learned that becoming a manager is not the end of the journey; it is the beginning of a new one. You have exchanged some of your duties of obedience for responsibilities. You have also learned that you don't have to have all the answers all the time but you still must treat your team members' questions with respect and thoughtfulness.

Finally, you have learned about getting noticed as a potential manager. This section may not have seemed that important to you if you have recently received your first promotion. But remember, it won't be long before you start looking for the next promotion, so keep the tips in mind. They will not only stand you in good stead for promotion but also help you to be a better manager now.

SUNDAY

MONDAY

TUESDAY

WEDNESDAY

THURSDAY

FRIDAY

SATURDAY

Tomorrow we will look at some of the principal focus points you will need to home in on as you make the transition from team member to team manager.

Fact-check (answers at the back)

1. The letters RHIP stand for...
   a) Really Helps Improve Performance ☐
   b) Rank Has Its Privileges ☐
   c) Right Here I'm Promoted ☐
   d) Respect Helps Intimidate People ☐

2. Which one of the following is *not* one of the eight responsibilities of a manager?
   a) To state the overall aims and norms of the team ☐
   b) To intimidate your team into doing what they're told ☐
   c) To formulate the plans for the team ☐
   d) To motivate the team, as a team, and on an individual basis ☐

3. What was the name of the book written by Niccolò Machiavelli?
   a) *The Prince* ☐
   b) *The Price* ☐
   c) *The Manager* ☐
   d) *The Place* ☐

4. As discussed in this chapter 'networking' is...
   a) Connecting computers together ☐
   b) Using social networking sites to connect with friends ☐
   c) Getting your name known among senior decision makers ☐
   d) Taking breaks to gossip to with people ☐

5. When a person asks a question you should use the '4 Ds' to respond. The '4 Ds' are...
   a) Delay, Defer, Deal or Deflect ☐
   b) Deride, Defer, Deal or Deflect ☐
   c) Despise, Delay, Deal or Defer ☐
   d) Dominate, Deal, Deflect or Delay ☐

6. What is the missing element in this equation: Luck = _____ + preparedness ?
   a) Opportunity ☐
   b) Effort ☐
   c) Action ☐
   d) Intelligence ☐

7. Who said 'The day soldiers stop bringing you their problems is the day you have stopped leading them'?
   a) Colin Powell ☐
   b) Colin Montgomery ☐
   c) Nelson Mandela ☐
   d) Winston Churchill ☐

8. Being promoted to the level of your incompetence is called the...
   a) Petra Principle ☐
   b) Paul Principle ☐
   c) Peter Principle ☐
   d) Pareto Principle ☐

9. *Noblesse oblige* means....
   a) People are obliged to treat me as a noble ☐
   b) With rank comes responsibility ☐
   c) Respect must be earned ☐
   d) Don't do anything without my blessing ☐

10. A paradigm is...
    a) A perception, view or attitude to something ☐
    b) The same as a paradox – a contradiction ☐
    c) The extra money that you get as a manager ☐
    d) A part-qualified manager ☐

MONDAY

Improve your focus

As a lowly employee you focus pretty much on one thing – what your boss asks, or tells, you to do. As a manager, you now have a whole lot of other things to focus on. You have to have a sound understanding of:

- your own targets and objectives
- your team's targets and objectives
- your team's workload
- individuals' workloads within the team
- individuals' and the team's capability
- daily, seasonal and market-led changes that can affect the team
- the commercial value of your team or at least the financial costs of your team's existence
- the activities that your team handles for the organization.

Without this understanding, you *may* be able to get by for a while, if everything remains stable. But you won't survive for long and you certainly won't *thrive* as a manager. If you lack this understanding, you will not be able to manage any form of change effectively; and remember, change doesn't have to come as a big, branded 'change programme' managed from head office. Your boss simply asking you and your team to take on some extra responsibilities, or to reduce your costs by 10 per cent, constitutes a significant enough change to leave a poor manager rapidly drowning.

Focus on your own targets and objectives

OK, this is too obvious for words, isn't it? Of course, you are still going to focus on your *own* targets and objectives; it was by doing that well that you got promoted to a management role. It's easy.

But, in fact, it isn't quite as easy as you might think. Some of your personal targets and objectives are new to you – those relating to:

● managing your team's performance
● managing grievances and disciplinary issues in your team
● collecting and collating Management Information (MI – specific information that management use to track performance such as sales, costs and productivity)
● reporting MI to your manager.

Some of the targets you used to get personally you will now be given as an overall target for you *and* your team; you are going to have to decide how to divide these targets up equitably; if you take on too much it will have two potential consequences:

1 You may bite off more than you can chew and thus you are setting yourself up to fail
2 You may end up in a situation that is known as MIYST – Managing In Your Spare Time.

Case study

Amil had recently been promoted as a team leader with four people reporting to him. He and his team were responsible for selling hotel rooms over the phone to incoming callers and to making response calls to warm leads. When setting the individual targets he felt that he should continue to lead by example and to prove himself. He set his personal target at 30 per cent of the team target and divided the remaining 70 per cent of the target between his four team members. Within six months it was clear that, though Amil was hitting his sales target, he was struggling to fulfil some of his other objectives. He had had

> to work the weekend at the end of every month to get his reports in on time, he had had to call staff in after hours to deal with problems that they reported, and he had only managed to hold the performance reviews with his team by doing them in the pub after work. He was, in short, stuck in MIYST.

Focus on your team's targets and objectives

If you run a sales team, then setting targets and objectives is relatively straightforward. It isn't necessarily easy, but there is at least a clear and logical set of numbers attached, whether it is sales units or income, gross revenue generated or profit. For instance:

You are to generate a minimum of £235,000 in invoiced margin over the next eight months (period end 31.07.20XX). 50 per cent of this figure may come from current clients and the other 50 per cent is to come from clients with whom we do not presently do business.

Always give an objective to an individual. If you use 'we', then no one really knows who exactly is accountable for achieving this objective

Similarly, if your people are working on projects it is again fairly straightforward to generate meaningful objectives. For instance:

You are to design a bridge structure for submission to the XYZ Company according to Contract Specification 20897. Initial design is to be fully submitted by the 31 July 20XX.

Or:

> *You are to repaint Rooms 4, 5 and 6, using Brilliant White emulsion on the ceilings, Rose Pink Vinyl silk on the walls and Off White gloss on the woodwork. Two coats on all surfaces. To be ready for the furnishing of the rooms by 09.00 on the morning of the 16 January 20XX.*

However, lots of people just have a job... No one ever sets them any targets or goals or objectives. Yes, it's hard to come up with a meaningful objective for someone who has a 'reactive' job such as the receptionist. But, without objectives, people tend to stagnate, so try really hard to find objectives for *everyone*.

Here are some examples of areas where you can set objectives for people who have reactive roles:

● **Personal development** You can set someone an objective to develop a skill, ability or area of knowledge, e.g.:

> *You are to attend a training course entitled 'Etes, Shutes and Levees' run by Clutterbuck and Co. as soon as possible but no later than 21 February 20XX.*

● **Performance improvement** You can set someone an objective to overcome a weakness, e.g.:

> *You are to ensure that your submitted reports over the next 12 months are completely free of any spelling or grammatical errors.*

● Or you can set a **combination** of the two above, e.g.:

> *A.* *You are to ensure that your submitted reports over the next 12 months are completely free of any spelling or grammatical errors.*

> *B.* *To help you to achieve this you are to attend a Training Course entitled 'Etes, Shutes and Levees' run by Clutterbuck and Co. as soon as possible but no later than 21 February 20XX.*

● **Development of their job** You can set someone an objective to find a way to improve their work output or service to their customers, e.g.:

> *Carry out a full inventory of the stationery store by the 21st of this month. Identify overstocks and make recommendations to reduce our stationery spend by a minimum of 20 per cent. Recommendations by the 30th of this month.*

● You can even set someone an objective to **identify some objectives** for themselves, e.g.:

> *You are to identify three SMART objectives for yourself to be achieved during the next six months. You are to present those to me for discussion at a one-hour meeting on Tuesday the 12 August 20XX.*

● You can set an objective that relates to a **proposed action** that hasn't yet been signed off, e.g.:

> *You are to read over and analyse the project plan and identify what a) challenges you perceive will need to be overcome and b) opportunities you can see to improve the plan. You should submit these discoveries in a brief written paper to be with me no later than 4 p.m. on the 23 January 20XX.*

● You can set an objective that anticipates a **change in working practices**, e.g.:

> *In order to increase the number of staff you support by two, without increasing your working hours, you need to report back in seven days with a list of tasks that you currently fulfil which you could pass to others. Annotate this list with an estimate of time saved. At that meeting, we will agree objectives for you to pass these tasks to appropriate others, ensuring that they are sufficiently skilled to take on the jobs.*

Before you talk to a team member about their targets and objectives, work out how SMART you have got them.

SMART

S **Specific:** What is it that you are going to *achieve* rather than simply *do*?

M **Measurable:** Can you measure either the total success or what proportion of success has been achieved?

A **Achievable:** There are two elements to this:

1 Can it actually be done?
2 Is it within the power of the person or of someone or something else?

Passing down unachievable targets used to be something that your boss did, and it didn't motivate you! Now *you* are the one passing down the objectives, so before you do ask yourself two questions:

1 Are these achievable targets?
2 Have I given the person the time, resources, support and skills to achieve them?

R **Relevant:** Is it actually this person's job to do this *and* does it move the department or organization forward?

T **Time-bound:** Have you set a specific time by which it is to be achieved?

Focus on your people's workloads and capability

It is also quite probable that some of your team may have other workloads: some may be project team members working part of their time on projects for other managers; some may be training new people, and others may not be full-time employees so they will have fewer hours to contribute.

You will need to look quite carefully at the way you divide up team targets and objectives between the people in the team. This will be relevant both at the beginning of a period and on a day-to-day basis as you set deadlines with people for small tasks.

Case study

Amil, having taken 30 per cent of the departmental sales target as his own, now divided the remaining 70 per cent equally between his four staff, However:

- Sunil was an experienced salesman and was born to sell

- Aparna was just out of college and still hadn't really learned how the systems worked

- Shilpa spent a lot of her time running the induction programmes for Amil's boss

- Vinod was more interested in texting his girlfriend than actually making sales calls

- Amil went for a simple, equal distribution that, while *equal*, may not have been at all *fair*.

It is unlikely that everyone in *your* team has equal levels of ability or expertise, so try to make sure that the targets are distributed fairly rather than purely equally. You may need to discuss this with team members to explain why the division is being set up the way it is; we will address this more on Tuesday, in the chapter about communication.

Focus on looking out for daily, seasonal and market-led changes

It is always a challenge to keep your eyes on the outside world; you have so many things to get on and do that you just don't have the time to stop and look around. If you don't though, you'll find that the world passes you by. Why does this matter?

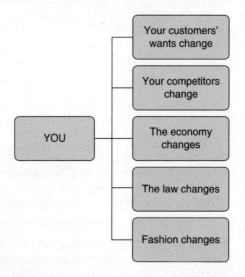

If you don't change, then you are going to get left behind!

You don't have to do all this by yourself, of course – you can set objectives for members of the team about keeping abreast with the changing situation. The Internet is a wonderful resource for this; almost every market sector has newsletters that regularly cover market updates.

SUNDAY
MONDAY
TUESDAY
WEDNESDAY
THURSDAY
FRIDAY
SATURDAY

TIP *Just put 'industry updates' into a search engine. I just got 642 million results and the first page alone stretches from biotech, electrical, medical, defence, airlines to healthcare!*

Focus on the 'value' of your team...

Focus on understanding what your team *contributes* to the organization as a whole. This may sound strange but there are very sound reasons. The pace of change in the world is probably faster now than at almost any time in recorded history. And the change is global. In the past it took decades or even centuries for a discovery in China to reach Europe or an invention in Africa to reach the USA; nowadays it happens in a matter of hours. Your team could be outsourced, or offshored, in no time at all; or even if the future isn't quite that bleak, your budget could be diverted to something or somewhere else.

As the manager, it is your job to defend your team, and you can do that only if you know what they bring to the table.

Case study

Robert was new to the team and had been drafted in as the new team leader. On his first day he asked questions such as 'What does the team generate in terms of revenue?', 'What are the costs of the team?' and, therefore, 'What contribution does the team make to the organization's financial health?'

He was amazed to find out that no one knew. No one had ever asked these questions before. Robert searched and analysed, dug out data and crunched numbers. He was just completing his quest when the word came down from the Board that his team's function 'no longer fitted with the strategy of the organization'. His team was to be disbanded and all the staff were to be let go. Robert was able to go to the Board and prove that, while the team

> may not *appear* to fit with the strategy, they did actually contribute approximately 15 per cent of the profitability of the company... The Board changed their mind!

Armed with this knowledge you are not only stronger to protect your team's interest from such extreme situations. In addition:

- you are able to better argue the case for more resources
- your credibility is higher when you want to propose new products, services or processes
- your team's self-confidence increases as they recognize that they are a key part of the organization, rather than a backroom function or an overhead.

If you work in a non-profit making organization – a local authority or a health provider for instance – then it may be more difficult to quantify what you and your team actually bring to the table. In this instance, try to identify the comparative 'return on investment' in whatever units are appropriate:

- 'We provide services to X,000 households.'
- 'We collect Y,000 tonnes of rubbish each year.'
- 'We carry out Z,000 operations each month.'

You are also well advised to carry out a comparison with other similar functions in other organizations to see how effective your team is in relation to others; compare the teams in terms of size, expenses, output and resources. For instance:

	Our team (The Personnel Department at Transport Union)	The Personnel Department at the Civil Aviation Bureau
Staff	6	9
Population supported	32	29
Payroll managed	$960,000	$970,000
No. of days training delivered	71	22
No. of disciplinaries this year	4	7

Conclusion:
We support a similar sized population and accurately manage a similar sized payroll with 66 per cent of the staff. We deliver more than three times the amount of in-house training.

Summary

Today you have learned about some of the factors required in making the transition from being a team member to being a team leader. You have learned that as a manager you have to have a different focus to someone who is solely a follower. You have learned about setting equitable objectives, and making sure they are SMART. You have also recognized the importance of keeping your eyes open to the ever-changing and evolving world.

You have additionally learned that your people don't all have the same level of capacity, and that as a manager it is your responsibility to recognize and allow for this. Finally, you have learned to measure the output and value of your team; this helps you to protect your team as well as raising your credibility when you ask for more resources or to change processes.

Tomorrow we will look at how to improve your communication – a vital area for any manager.

SUNDAY

MONDAY

TUESDAY

WEDNESDAY

THURSDAY

FRIDAY

SATURDAY

Fact-check (answers at the back)

1. What does the 'S' stand for in MIYST?
   a) Standing ❑
   b) Spare ❑
   c) Strong ❑
   d) Sweet ❑

2. What does SMART stand for?
   a) Specific, Mine, Achievable, Relevant, Time-bound ❑
   b) Simple, Measurable, Achievable, Relevant, Time-bound ❑
   c) Specific, Mine, Achievable, Reasonable, Time-bound ❑
   d) Specific, Measurable, Actionable, Relevant, Time-bound ❑

3. What is wrong with the following objective: 'We must increase sales by 10 per cent by the end of the current quarter'?
   a) We can't increase sales; there is a recession on ❑
   b) 10 per cent is too high ❑
   c) No single person is responsible for this ❑
   d) 10 per cent is too low ❑

4. If a person doesn't have objectives, they tend to...
   a) Stagnate ❑
   b) Achieve well ❑
   c) Do nothing at all ❑
   d) Fail ❑

5. As a manager, it is important that you stay aware of changes in...
   a) Your competitors ❑
   b) Your customers' wants ❑
   c) The economy ❑
   d) All of the above ❑

6. Targets and workload should always be divided between the team...
   a) Equally ❑
   b) Fairly ❑
   c) Randomly ❑
   d) According to whom you like the most ❑

7. Why do you need to understand the value of your team/department to the organization?
   a) In order to protect their interests ❑
   b) It adds to your credibility when seeking extra resources ❑
   c) Neither a) nor b) ❑
   d) Both a) and b) ❑

8. If you can't 'value' your team by revenue generated, which of the following is a strong way to assess their value to the organization?
   a) The number of people in the team ❑
   b) The size of your team budget ❑
   c) The number of customers/clients your team services ❑
   d) The size of your office ❑

9. If the team doesn't change it will get...
a) ...left behind ❏
b) ...stronger ❏
c) ...bigger ❏
d) ...better ❏

10. In SMART, 'Achievable' has two elements. Which of the following is an accurate summary of both?
a) It can be done and it can be done by the person asked to do it ❏
b) It can be done and it can be done easily ❏
c) It can be done and you could do it, so you can expect a member of your team to do it ❏
d) If a person is prepared to make enormous sacrifices, they can do it ❏

TUESDAY

Improve your communication

Large organizations and professional institutes frequently carry out surveys into the opinions of their staff and members. If a survey asks 'What could be done to improve your day-to-day working environment?', the subject of communication nearly always comes up!

When you look below the surface of the answers, there are many different facets:

- Sometimes people feel that they are kept in the dark and don't get enough information.
- Sometimes people feel that they are swamped with information and simply cannot sort what they need to know from what they could do without.
- Sometimes the issue is about timing – they only get to know things when it is almost too late to do anything.
- Sometimes it is about the medium – they get a formal letter when a quiet chat would have been more appropriate.
- Sometimes it is about the *passage* of the message – if they feel that the message was so important or controversial that it should have come direct from the chief executive, but they were told by a junior HR manager, they are upset by this.

As a manager, it is vital that you make sure that your communication skills are as good as possible; otherwise, you are just making your job harder.

What is 'communication'?

Communication is a vital human skill and an even more important skill for anyone who wishes to lead or manage others. Real communication involves two aspects:

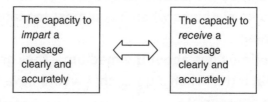

The capacity to *impart* a message clearly and accurately	⟺	The capacity to *receive* a message clearly and accurately

Capacity in this instance means both ability and motivation.

Towers Watson's *2011/2012 Change and Communication ROI Survey* pinpointed four specific traits of better managers:

1 Better managers are authentic in their delivery of messages.
2 Better managers are transparent in their messages to employees.
3 Better managers create a dialogue with employees.
4 Better managers make themselves accessible and responsive to employee questions and suggestions.

In fact, the survey results show that better managers are about three times better at these things than less effective managers!

Leaders at my organization are:

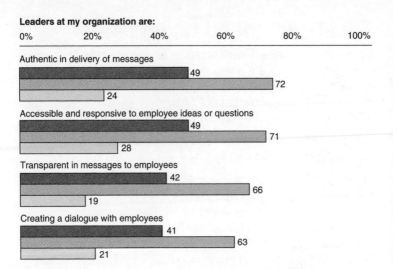

0%   20%   40%   60%   80%   100%

Authentic in delivery of messages
49
72
24

Accessible and responsive to employee ideas or questions
49
71
28

Transparent in messages to employees
42
66
19

Creating a dialogue with employees
41
63
21

■ Overall ■ High communication effectiveness □ Low communication effectiveness

Source: **Towers Watson's** *2011/2012 Change and Communication ROI Survey*

What does this mean to you as a manager?

1 You need to ensure that *you* have the capacity to both impart messages and receive messages effectively, *and...*

2 As the manager, it is now *your responsibility* to ensure that your team has both of these capacities as well. This may mean providing team members with training or managing their motivation to both speak up and to listen and react.

Facets you need to get right

Let's consider the different facets of communication that you need to try to get right if you are to be a better manager. What appears below is a list of facets; they aren't necessarily in the most appropriate order but the order they are in spells out the word 'COMMIT', which may help you to remember them.

Content

Think about what you actually need to include in this communication; do you need to tell everyone everything? Or would some people be better off with a précis of the information? There is a text-speak acronym that has become popular over the past few years, TMI – which stands for 'Too Much Information' – and much workaday communication falls into this category. You may need to reduce the quantity of data you include for reasons of the recipients' workload or capacity to take it in:

- Senior executives usually demand an 'executive summary' on a lengthy report giving just the most pertinent data
- People who work shifts or are on piecework usually get reduced data simply because longwinded communiqués take up too much of their shift or earning time
- Sometimes the whole story is just too complex for some people and so they benefit from being told only what immediately impacts them.

On the other hand, *not* providing information to people presents a different problem:

> **'An individual without information cannot take responsibility; an individual who is given information cannot help but take responsibility.'**
>
> Jan Carlzon (former chairman of SAS Airlines),
> *Moments of Truth* (HarperCollins, 1989)

So the better manager strikes a balance between swamping people with information and keeping people in the dark.

Other people

You need to take into consideration the other people with whom you are communicating:

● **Do they speak your language?** We aren't just looking at the difference between English and Gujarati, but the difference between British English and American English, e.g.:

> *In British English someone might say 'Do you want me to knock you up in the morning?', meaning 'wake you up'.*

> *In American English, someone is 'knocked up' if they are expecting a baby.*

● There are also **differences in language between organizations**, e.g.:

> *In a mechanical engineering company a 'workshop' is full of machines, tools and engineers.*

> *In a college a workshop is a training session for students.*

● There are also differences between levels in the hierarchy; management jargon can get a bit silly at times, e.g.:

> *A training company in the UK received an enquiry as to whether they provided a training course in 'cross business unit internal mobility'. They had no idea what the buying manager wanted, so they emailed back and asked. The response that came back said that they didn't know either but this was what the line manager had asked them to source!*

Method

There are various options open to you in the 21st century:

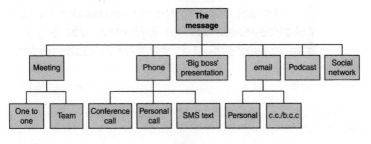

43

Your challenge is to make sure that you *deliberately* pick the right method (or combination of methods) for getting the message across. You should bear in mind that, if you want to be a better manager, you must also ensure that you create the right environment for people to come back with questions or suggestions.

Messenger

Your boss will often expect you to 'cascade' messages down to your team, and this is part of what you are paid for. Sometimes, however, it is more appropriate for your boss, or even your boss's boss, to communicate directly with your team.

Case studies

Nigel was a senior executive who instigated a strategy with the Board of a 10 per cent reduction in headcount. He passed the word to his departmental managers that they needed to pass this message on to the shop floor. While all the individual managers broke the news effectively, people on the shop floor felt that Nigel was hiding behind the 'chain of command' in a cowardly way; he hadn't the nerve to tell them in person. Morale plummeted.

Jane, the Managing Director of the same company, got a very nice letter from a very important client to say thank you to several named individuals after a particularly challenging project was completed. Rather than pass the message down the hierarchy, she left her office and went round the building seeking out the individuals and telling them personally of her thanks and admiration. Her reputation rose enormously, even though most staff didn't actually see her for months on end.

Intention

Before you make any attempt to communicate with people, ask yourself what your intention is. Are you informing someone of something solely so that they know? Or are you expecting them to do something as a result of this? This is often seen in meeting minutes as two columns on the right side of the page headed 'Information' and 'Action'. When a person's initials appear in the 'Information' column they know that they are simply being made aware, whereas when their initials appear in the 'Action' column they know that they actually have to do something. In the former case, so long as they understand the message then the job is done. In the latter case, you may need to make much more effort to ensure that the person understands all the SMART aspects of the action they need to take.

You can continue this idea of Information/Action in the 'Subject' line of emails.

Timing

Always consider the timing of any communication in two different areas:

1 **Comparative timing** Are you telling everyone at the same time or will some people get to know before others?
   - If you communicate with people at different times, ask yourself what effect this might have on both them and you. Might people be upset to discover that they were the last to know?
   - If you are entering into a dialogue about an issue, is it possible that you will give people the impression that you are swayed by the people you have already spoken to and listened to?
2 **Positioning of the communication** What else is happening at the same time?
   - Picking a Friday afternoon, just as people go home for the weekend, is not a good time to break bad news, as they will worry about it over their weekend.
   - Neither is it a good idea to give much needed good news at a time when everyone's mind is elsewhere. Trying to get the Finance Director to listen to a budget request at the time that the Finance Department is trying to submit the annual report figures is almost doomed to failure.

3 So think about the timing of meetings and the arrival of emails but don't become as cynical as some people:

Case study

At 14:55 UK time on 11 September 2001, after both World Trade Center towers had been hit in the terror attacks, but before either tower had collapsed, a UK civil servant sent an email to the press office of her department that read: 'It's now a very good day to get out anything we want to bury. Councillors' expenses?'

This email ultimately cost her her job.

Summary

Today we have looked at the most important elements of communication. Frankly, we could devote an entire library to the topic – it is that important! We have addressed the fact that a better manager not only 'talks the talk' but is also able to *listen*.

Communication isn't just about the 'big' messages. It is about the day-to-day matters of people's work – What are they expected to do? How are they doing? And what do they need?

To be a better manager you need to communicate with your boss as well as your team, so you will find yourself in the middle, acting as a conduit for messages passing up and down the chain of command. Make sure that you act as an intelligent conduit, not just a messenger. Remember the COMMIT acronym and make judgements that will help your team to understand your message.

In many roles, the ability to communicate effectively is the single greatest key to success and this is very true of management roles. So I strongly recommend that you take a

SUNDAY
MONDAY
TUESDAY
WEDNESDAY
THURSDAY
FRIDAY
SATURDAY

'lifelong learning' approach to communication and constantly strive to improve your own abilities and those of your team.

Tomorrow we will focus on how you can develop your team over the longer term.

Fact-check (answers at back)

1. According to Towers Watson's 2011/2012 survey, better managers...
a) Are authentic in their delivery of messages ☐
b) Are transparent in their messages to employees ☐
c) Create a dialogue with employees ☐
d) Do all of the above ☐

2. We defined 'communication' as involving two aspects. What are they?
a) The capacity to impart and receive a message clearly and accurately ☐
b) The capacity to create and impart a message clearly and accurately ☐
c) The capacity to receive and interpret a message clearly and accurately ☐
d) The capacity to listen ☐

3. Your boss should give your staff a message directly (rather than 'cascading' it down through you) in which situation?
a) Never ☐
b) When the boss wants to ☐
c) When the message would be better coming direct ☐
d) Only when you aren't in the workplace ☐

4. When considering your 'Intention' in the COMMIT acronym, you should be deciding whether you are telling a person for reasons of...
a) Information and/or Action ☐
b) Intelligence and/or Action ☐
c) Intelligence and/or Auditing ☐
d) Information and/or Auditing ☐

5. Giving people 'bad news' on a Friday afternoon, just before they go home is a...
a) Good idea – it means they can't ask questions about it ☐
b) Good idea – they can discuss it with their families ☐
c) Bad idea – as they will worry about it over the weekend ☐
d) Bad idea – as they might call you at home with questions ☐

6. TMI in this instance stands for...
a) Too Much Information ☐
b) This Memo's Important ☐
c) Tell Me Immediately ☐
d) Team Members – Important! ☐

7. If people don't have *enough* information they...
a) Cannot take responsibility for their actions or inactions ☐
b) Will probably do something 'wrong' ☐
c) May do nothing for fear of doing something wrong ☐
d) All of the above ☐

8. Hiding something unpleasant in an unrelated 'big story' may...
a) Be a great way to bury bad news ❏
b) May have even more unpleasant repercussions ❏
c) Is not entirely ethical ❏
d) All of the above ❏

9. What is 'cross business unit internal mobility'?
a) I have no idea ❏
b) It relates to angry department heads ❏
c) It relates to selling services between departments ❏
d) It relates to people moving to another company ❏

10. We identified three ways to use the phone to communicate with people. What were these?
a) Personal call, conference call and SMS text message ❏
b) Mobile, landline and VOIP ❏
c) Scheduled call, impromptu call and long call ❏
d) Quick chat, video call and voicemail ❏

SUNDAY

MONDAY

TUESDAY

WEDNESDAY

THURSDAY

FRIDAY

SATURDAY

WEDNESDAY

Improving
your team
members,
including
yourself

In his book *Seven Habits of Highly Effective People*, the late Dr Stephen Covey summed up his definition of effectiveness in his notion of the 'P/PC Balance', where:

- **P = production** the ability to produce results and output *today* – this is most probably seen in your team by the activity and achievement of daily, weekly or monthly targets
- **PC = production capacity** the ability to continue to produce results in the more distant future – this is probably more realistically measured in somewhere between one and five years.

'Improving your team members, including yourself' stands squarely on the PC side of the balance.

As a manager, it is part of your responsibility to ensure that you and your team are capable of being productive in the future. We have already mentioned this in previous chapters: on Sunday we met it when we introduced the 'Peter Principle'; on Monday we met it when looking at setting objectives for people, and on Tuesday we touched on it when we identified that as a manager you have the responsibility to ensure that your team can communicate effectively. So let's now look at the topic in more detail.

What is it that you can improve?

It is important to recognize that 'improving' covers a wide range of areas:

- increasing an individual's **knowledge**
- learning a **skill** new to the individual
- getting better at an **existing skill**
- making an existing skill **more habitual** and therefore **easier** to do
- understanding the **need** for the use of a skill, behaviour or knowledge.

Why should you try to improve people?

Improvement may be required for a wide variety of reasons:

- to raise the value that the individual offers to you (as their manager) and the organization
- to raise the individual's morale and self-esteem
- to turn around poor performance
- to allow you to allocate workloads more equitably
- to help you to spend less time having to supervise and monitor people because they are capable and motivated
- to enable people to become multi-skilled, which in turn has three main improvement outcomes:
  - it allows you greater flexibility when allocating workloads
  - it allows people greater flexibility with shifts and holidays
  - it gives people more variety and therefore less chance of getting bored
- simply to keep up with technological advances in your industry
- to keep ahead of the competition
- to keep up with the ever-growing expectations of customers.

With regard to the final three bullets in the list above, it is worth noting that if you don't improve, the world will simply pass you by.

How can you help people improve?

1 **Select people who have an appropriate level of ambition and potential.** This means that when you recruit you must be realistic about the medium-term prospects for the people who join you. There is little point in recruiting graduates or highly intelligent people to undertake a role that requires no thought; they will soon become bored and unproductive. Similarly, if the role is one that requires intellect and dedication, then there is little point in recruiting less educated/intelligent people simply because they are cheap!

2 **Practise effective delegation.** Delegating responsibility for fulfilling a task is an efficient way to develop a person's ability, skill and motivation:
   - It proves that they can do it – both to you and to themselves.
   - It frees you up to do other things and from having to oversee them.
   - It raises their standing among their peers as they are seen to be trusted.

3 **Use 'training' efficiently.** The less effective manager takes the view that sending someone on a training course is a silver bullet that will suddenly result in a massive improvement in performance. A better manager realizes that there are steps that he or she needs to take in order to make any training course as effective as possible:

a) Identify *exactly* what it is that the person will be able to do differently, or know, after the training, that they don't do, or know, now. Avoid general concepts such as 'to get better at time management', and go for specific elements such as 'to learn how to avoid distractions and therefore be more able to hit deadlines'.

b) Discuss this with the individual so they have the same expectation as you. If the person thinks that you are sending them to training for a different reason from the actual reason, it can create problems. If they think it is a punishment when it isn't, it makes them resentful; if they think it is a reward when it isn't, it tends to prevent them from learning.

c) Provide them with training relevant to their needs and that is suitable for their personal style. If someone simply needs to learn how to spell, don't send them on a whole language course; if the person is not very intellectual, don't send them on a four-day classroom-based mini MBA.

d) When they have completed the training, discuss with them what they learned and how they will put it into practice in the workplace. If you don't do this, you look as if you don't care how the course went and what they got out of it. If you don't care, why should they?

e) Support them over the following months to help them make the new knowledge or skill a habit at work. Support can include constantly reminding them of their new-found ability; giving them better tools to match their skills; and giving them greater responsibility to allow them to put their new skills to good use.

4 Recognize that 'training' is not the only way in which people can improve. Training is probably one of the more expensive ways in which you can help people to improve their knowledge and skills, so a better manager uses a full range of methods to achieve the goal of learning and performance improvement:

- E-learning may be available to you through the organization or just by a private download from the Internet.
- Self-help books – let's face it, you are reading one right this minute!
- YouTube has an enormous number of 'how to'-type videos available on subjects ranging from making presentations to managing negative people.
- E-guides for smartphones are available as e-books.
- Podcasts.
- A person can 'shadow' someone who is using the sorts of skills that they need to learn.

- You can send a person or a group on a study tour; this could be in your own organization or with a client or customer.
- One of the most effective ways to get a person to really understand a subject is to get them to teach it to others. Set a task to learn all they can about a topic and then provide short lessons to the rest of the team.
- Put them 'in at the deep end' – just give them a task that they have never done before and see how they do. Make it clear that the idea is for them to learn and not that you are deliberately setting them up to fail!

> ### *'I am always doing that which I cannot do, in order that I may learn how to do it.'*
> Pablo Picasso

5 **Coach people supportively.** Coaching is not about teaching someone. It is a process whereby you, as a coach, ask them the right questions in order to get them to think of the answers and solutions to their own issues. Coaching is not appropriate for everyone and in all situations but it may be a good way to identify which solution may suit the individual best. For example by asking the right type of open questions you may be able to get the individual to find the most effective method from the list in point number 4 above.

Improve your team rather than doing their jobs for them

In a short book entitled *The One Minute Manager Meets the Monkey* (Harper, 2011), Ken Blanchard uses the analogy that a problem or issue is like a pet monkey – it needs to be looked after until it is dealt with. Many employees are very adept at giving their monkeys to their manager. Let's explore this analogy through a case study:

Case study

Helen is a manager and Wayne is a member of her team. Wayne has to produce a report each week and send it to the Finance Department. Wayne comes to see Helen and says, 'Hi, Helen, I've done the report, but could you just check it over before it goes off to the Finance Director?' Helen is busy but she is also a supportive manager, so she replies, 'No problem, leave it on my desk and I'll take a look as soon as I've finished this.'

Now, the responsibility for *checking* the report is Helen's, so is the responsibility for getting it to the Finance Director on time. Wayne has effectively given Helen the monkey... She is now doing his job as well as her own.

Monkeys can also be passed on when something unusual happens:

Wayne has to rely on Kurt to supply him with data to input into the report he produces for the Finance Department. Kurt has recently started to provide the information late or in a wrong format and Wayne is now having to spend a lot of time chasing Kurt. Wayne goes to Helen and tells her that Kurt is making his life difficult. When Helen asks Wayne if he has asked Kurt to provide the information 'properly', he replies, 'No, I find him intimidating, and it isn't my job to chase him!.'

Helen agrees that she will speak to Kurt and make sure that he provides the data to Wayne on time in the future.

Helen has both taken on Wayne's monkey – he should be developing the ability to deal assertively with Kurt – and prevented him from developing this skill.

As you can imagine, if Helen has four people reporting to her, and they are all as good at handing her their monkeys, Helen's life is going to rapidly become unmanageable. So what should Helen have done in each case?

When Wayne asked, 'Hi, Helen, I've done the report, but could you just check it over before it goes off to the Finance Director?' she could have replied: 'Wayne, I'm glad you have done it in good time. Have you checked it over yourself?' If he hasn't, then he should go and do so – that is his job. If he has, then she should ask, 'So why do you want *me* to check it *again*, do you think that there is a problem with it?'

At this stage Wayne will probably recognize that he is asking her to do something that is unnecessary. If there is no problem, then Helen can tell him that she has faith in his professionalism and he can submit it when he is ready. If he says that there *is* a problem, then Helen should agree a time for them to look at it *together*. The problem and the solution remain Wayne's but he has Helen's help.

In the second situation when Wayne admitted that he finds Kurt intimidating Helen should have asked what it was about Kurt that had this effect. This would start Wayne thinking about his capacity to be assertive and the likely results if Kurt thought that he had run to Helen as soon as he faced a problem.

If Helen didn't have the time to have this discussion with Wayne when he raised it, she should have set a meeting time to discuss it.

Give feedback

People can't improve if they don't know *how* they are doing. Do you remember the quote in the last chapter? 'An individual without information cannot take responsibility; an individual

who is given information cannot help but take responsibility.'
In short: If I don't know I'm doing it wrong, I'll never be able to do it right!

Better managers give people feedback, not once a year at the annual appraisal, or even once a month, at a group meeting or a one-to-one, but *every day*. Feedback to people doesn't have to be a big event; it can just be a little, 'well done' or a 'thank you', a 'that was good' or a 'nice work'. Feedback should always be timely – that is, as soon after the performance to which it relates as possible. Feedback should also be delivered in a suitable environment, one where the team member isn't going to be embarrassed in front of their peers (unless you expressly want to achieve this for a justifiable reason).

When performance wasn't so great, ask questions rather than just offering your judgement:

Case study

Helen: Wayne, that report you wrote, did you check it over before you sent it?

Wayne: No, I didn't have time.

Helen: OK, can you look it over now and see whether there are errors in it that you would have noticed if you had checked it?

Wayne: All right.

Sometime later...

Helen: Did you find any errors?

Wayne: Yes, lots, I'm afraid to say.

Helen: Do you think that the Finance Director was impressed with it?

Wayne: No, I doubt that very much.

Helen: What will you do next week to avoid this happening again?

Wayne: I'll make sure I've got the report written in time to check it before I send it.

Helen: Good man!

Receive feedback

Traditionally, a manager *received* feedback once a year, at his or her annual appraisal, and that feedback came from the manager's boss. How does a manager's boss evaluate the manager who reports to him or her? Solely on the basis of the reporting manager's achievement of targets, not on their management of their people. The result of this was that managers often progressed up the corporate ladder by being heartless slave-drivers rather than better managers.

A better manager cares about the opinion of the people he or she manages. That isn't to say that good managers should engage in popularity contests – you don't have to have your people love you – but you do want to be sure that, although they respect you, they don't hate you or fear you either.

You only get to hear people's opinions of your management style if you ask them and create an environment where they know that they can be honest and open with you without fear of reprisal.

Here are 10 steps to help you:

1 **Recognize reality.** No one is perfect, but you don't have to be bad to want to get better.
2 **Ask the 'right' people.** Choose people who:
   – have sufficient interaction with you to have a genuine opinion based on most of your work, rather than one tiny bit that they see

- have focus on problem solving, rather than being gossipmongers.

3 **Offer them a choice.** Give them the option to say no – they may be scared that you will hold any implied criticism against them.

4 **Ask the volunteer(s) to prepare.** A good way of doing this is to ask them to think about specific things that they would highlight using the grid below:

What do I do well/ that you respect?	What could I do better? (Don't expect them to tell you how you could do it better – that's your job!)
What should I do more of?	What should I do less of (or stop)?

5 **Suggest a suitable location.** Go for neutral ground; not your office. Go for somewhere relatively public, but not too noisy; coffee shops are generally quite good for this kind of conversation.

6 **Schedule sensibly.** Don't do this exercise outside work hours. Allow enough time to settle in, to get to the heart of the matters brought up, and to summarize at the end. Give yourself enough time afterwards to assimilate what's been said, rather than running straight on to the next meeting.

7 **Clarify expectations.** Explain why you want the feedback and assure the person that you are willing to change and that the feedback they give is the catalyst for this. Be honest and open about how long it may take to make some changes habitual; don't raise expectations that you will be able to improve overnight.

8 **Agree what you will do next**. If you are going to get feedback from several people, do this *before* you prioritize the changes you want to make. Share this prioritization with the people from whom you have received feedback. Agree any support you need from them.

Case study

A manager received feedback that he never listened properly and usually cut people off before they had even finished telling him something. He agreed to try to change this, but recognized that he would need constant reminders. In order that it didn't appear that his staff were criticizing him in public, he agreed a non-verbal signal that would tell him to shut up and listen. The signal was simply that, if he saw one of his team touch their ear, that was his cue to close his mouth. It worked and no one lost face.

9 **Show your appreciation.** You have asked your people to go out on a limb and trust you, so make sure they know that you appreciate it, and encourage them to approach you with further constructive feedback at any time,

10 **Go back to work and get better!**

Summary

Today we learned that constantly striving to improve is the only way to assure success, for individuals, teams and organizations. The key to improvement is knowledge – knowing how you are doing and knowing that you can get better at it. We learned that the best way for people, including ourselves, to know how they are doing is by receiving feedback. We learned how to *give* feedback – a crucial skill for many managers – and how to *receive* it – a crucial skill for any human being.

We learned that 'training' isn't something that we can leave exclusively to the Training Department; we as managers have a critical role to play as well.

There are four basic principles to remember about improving people:

- It should be a daily activity.
- It doesn't have to cost a lot of money.
- No one is perfect – everyone can improve.
- You don't have to be *bad* to want to get better.

Tomorrow we are going to look at a method for mapping and improving processes.

SUNDAY
MONDAY
TUESDAY
WEDNESDAY
THURSDAY
FRIDAY
SATURDAY

Fact-check (answers at back)

1. In Stephen Covey's definition of effectiveness, he refers to the 'P/PC Balance'. What does PC stand for?
   a) Political Correctness ❏
   b) Production Capacity ❏
   c) Promoted Competence ❏
   d) Perceived Competence ❏

2. A better manager knows that there are steps that he or she needs to take in order to make any training course as effective as possible. What is the first step?
   a) Identify *exactly* what it is that the person will be able to do differently, or know, after the training ❏
   b) Book a course ❏
   c) Tell the HR Department to book a course ❏
   d) Search the Internet for a 'how to' guide ❏

3. Which of the following was *not* mentioned as a reason to seek to improve people?
   a) To raise the individual's morale and self-esteem ❏
   b) To turn around poor performance ❏
   c) As a punishment for poor performance ❏
   d) To allow you to allocate workloads more equitably ❏

4. Complete the quote by the painter Pablo Picasso: 'I am always doing that which I cannot do...'.
   a) '...because I can do so little.' ❏
   b) '...because I believe I can do anything.' ❏
   c) '...in order that I may learn how to do it.' ❏
   d) '...in order to paint it.' ❏

5. If you put someone 'in at the deep end', what should you be sure that you do?
   a) Make it clear that you are sure that they will fail so they know that you have low expectations ❏
   b) Make it clear that you are not setting them up to fail ❏
   c) Watch them very closely and take over the minute they seem to be having difficulty ❏
   d) Leave them to it and then applaud them regardless of whether they succeed or fail ❏

6. Who meets the monkey in the title of a book by Ken Blanchard?
   a) The Dummy ❏
   b) The Time Manager ❏
   c) The One Minute Manager ❏
   d) The Better Manager ❏

7. In Step 6 of the guide to receiving feedback you were recommended to schedule sensibly. Particularly this told you:
a) To arrange the meeting out of hours ❏
b) To arrange the meeting to take up one hour ❏
c) To arrange the meeting back to back with other meetings ❏
d) To arrange the meeting in work hours ❏

8. When getting people to give you feedback it is suggested to go for neutral ground rather than your office. Why do you think this is?
a) Your office is *your* territory – this may be intimidating for a person ❏
b) You are only a junior manager – your office is probably too small ❏
c) You want to buy them a coffee so a coffee shop is better ❏
d) They are less likely to be prepared to upset you somewhere public ❏

9. Better managers give people feedback...
a) Once a year at their appraisal ❏
b) Once a month at a formal one-to-one ❏
c) Once a week in front of the whole team ❏
d) Every day, as appropriate to the person's performance ❏

10. Better managers seek feedback from people in their team in order to...
a) Know who doesn't like them ❏
b) Help them to improve their management ability ❏
c) Give the impression that they care what their subordinates think ❏
d) Train their staff in the giving of feedback ❏

THURSDAY

Improve your processes

We all use 'processes' in our everyday work, whether you manufacture cars or authorize mortgage applications, serve customers in a shop, or paint office buildings. Almost all jobs are made up of a series of repeated and repeatable actions that produce outputs.

Many of these processes have been arrived at by evolutionary means and have not been deliberately planned. They are the result of many years of intelligent, considered, but disjointed, thought. Sometimes processes were planned but they were planned a long time ago and the people, places, technology and customers have changed since the planning was done.

Consequently, many of our day-to-day processes fulfil our needs but are not necessarily as efficient and effective as they could or should be.

Today we will look at how by mapping processes we can fully understand them. After that we will cover the sensible steps that we can follow in order to identify, test and embed improvements – all with the intention of making life easier for you and your team.

Mapping processes

Process mapping is a tool that produces a diagrammatic representation of a process using standardized flowcharting symbols. This allows the process to be:

- easily explained to people new to the process
- broken down by activity, responsibility, ownership, dependency, concurrency and value
- assessed for bottlenecks and critical paths
- measured for time and resource usage

...all of which helps us to identify opportunities to improve the process.

Before you can start to map a process, you need to identify the product, service or outcome of the process. This may sound completely obvious but consider this:

> *If your team picks orders in a warehouse, is the outcome of the process the complete order sitting in a pile at the end of a conveyor belt? Or is it the order safely and securely packed in a box? Or does the box have to be addressed and labelled ready to go out of the door? Or do you have to send the dispatch note to accounts as well?*

Unless you are already the Managing Director, you will probably need to map processes at a 'micro level' – a micro-level process map shows individual steps such as 'Book interview rooms' and 'Send letters of appointment' or 'Print brochures' and 'Set up exhibition stand'. Note that:

- the boundaries of a micro-level process map are usually the physical boundaries of a team or a department;
- micro-level process maps really show up the detail, so these are the most commonly created when improving processes.

Symbols and conventions

There is a lot of software available (including shareware, freeware and add-ons to MS packages such as Excel) that can make process mapping or flowcharting very straightforward.

MS Project can produce flowcharts or PERT charts as well (look in 'View').

Alternatively, if your team aren't great IT users, you can use traditional methods – either by drawing it all with a pencil or creating it all with sticky notes and string (see below).

Normally, we map from left to right because that is the way we read and write in English, but, for ease of mapping on computers, many organizations map from top to bottom as this allows a reader to scroll down the process on screen rather than having arrows going back from the right of the page to the left.

The most common symbols are:

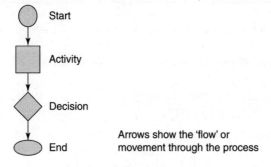

Start

Activity

Decision

End

Arrows show the 'flow' or movement through the process

You can use these easily if you are simply using pen and paper, but if you want to use a PC these symbols are available to pretty much everyone in Microsoft Word in the 'Draw' toolbar under 'AutoShapes' and 'Flowchart' and the 'Arrow' button.

The next few pages contain some words of advice about the usage of the basic symbols; these are useful whether you are using software or paper:

Starting out

It is critical to formally agree, and document, the point at which the mapped process starts. Thus, in the scenario of making a cup of tea, does the process start at the point when the kettle boils, or when the decision to have tea is made? This is important because you might be mapping a part of a larger process to which you only have access to the part that is done in your department or by your team; it will need to be clear that you haven't gone into detail on the bits *before* and *after* your process.

Activities

An activity is any step in the process where something happens or is done which furthers the process.

Where a macro-level process map may have activities grouped together under one heading – e.g. 'produce documents':

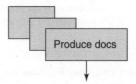

a micro-level process map will have the specific activities required to produce each of these documents listed in detail. A situation where there are several sub-processes happening at the same time is referred to as a **concurrency**. For example:

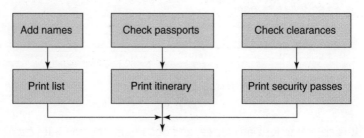

Where the process passes from person-to-person, the activities may be colour coded or grouped to show departmental, team or individual responsibility:

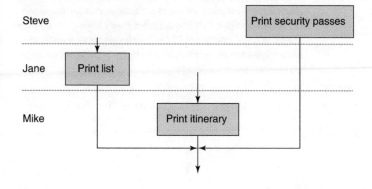

Decisions

Every decision inserted into a process map must be set as a closed question with a possible 'Yes' or 'No' answer. For example:

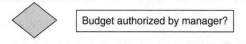

If 'Yes', the process moves on to the next stage; if 'No', the map must show what the next stage should be in that case:

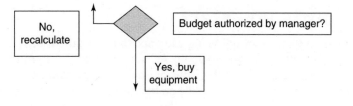

TIP *Don't miss out the decisions when mapping! Inserting decisions into a process map often highlights problem areas or improvement opportunities – often the activity is relatively quick but the output then waits for a supervisor or manager to make a decision that the output is ready to go on to the next stage. Having decisions listed on the process map also encourages the recognition of the effects of different decisions.*

NOTE: 'Activities' and 'Decisions' (and sometimes 'Movement') are often referred to generically as 'events' within the process.

Movement

The arrows show the onward movement of the 'product' through the string of events that make up the whole process.

The end point

The end point, like the start point, needs to be formally agreed. As in the earlier example, the end point may be a final product but it is just as likely that your end point is someone else's start point:

> *If your team picks orders in a warehouse, and the end point of your process is the complete order, safely and securely packed in a box, then another team will undoubtedly be required to take that end product, address and label it, and arrange courier collection and client invoicing.*

Before you start mapping

Before you actually get going you need to make sure that you know whether you are mapping 'As Is' or 'Should Be'. In most organizations, there is the 'official way' things **should be** done, and 'the way we actually do things' because it is quicker/easier/more responsive.

People often use a shortcut process in order to cut out delay and bureaucracy. While the shortcut seems to be sensible, they don't try to get this 'As Is' process recognized formally as 'Should Be' because they fear management delay to the changes or even criticism of the change.

When there is an accident, a problem or a complaint, because people are not using the 'Should Be' process, they can be held culpable (even without assessment of whether the laid-down process would have prevented the issue). This is most prevalent in cases of health and safety or unfair discrimination.

Let's look at an example to explore this distinction a little further.

Case study

'Should Be'

An IT consultancy had a process for setting up for newly hired employees. After a job offer was accepted the following process was laid down:

- The offer required authorization forms signed by a director.

- These were then sent to HR and Facilities to ensure that the individual was added to the payroll and allocated a desk.

- Once the desk had been allocated, more forms were sent from Facilities to IT to get networking cabling installed/checked and to ensure that software appropriate to the job was in place.

- Once the forms arrived in IT they were prioritized and added to the 'to do' list and budgets were allocated.

The problem was that there were many people involved in the chain from differing departments with other, competing priorities. IT consultancy is a fast-moving business and often new employees arrived fewer than 10 days after a job offer.

'As Is'

What actually used to happen was that as soon as an offer was accepted the hiring manager would phone Tom in IT and Tom would get straight on to it because Tom focused on helping his internal customer, rather than following a bureaucratic process that was laid down in the Standard Operating Procedures (SOPs).

No one changed the 'Should Be' because everyone got by on the 'As Is', until... Tom went away on holiday. Then a manager, finding that his new hire had arrived but that there was no PC for the guy to use, went to a local computer shop and bought a new PC over the counter on his company credit card.

Both the Facilities and Finance departments were livid that 'proper process' had not been followed, and the manager with the credit card bill got a roasting. He complained that the Facilities and Finance departments were holding up the 'real business of the company' and so it ended up as a Board-level issue!

'Should Be' processes are the ones that are usually found in the Standard Operating Procedures (SOPs), quality manuals, company policies, employee handbooks, HSE guidelines, procedures manuals and so on.

So long as we all understand whether we are looking at an 'As Is' process map or a 'Should Be' process map, we can continue. Where we are dealing with existing processes, especially ones that cross departmental boundaries and ones that are already described in a quality manual, procedures manual, set of SOPs or similar, it is often best to map both 'As Is' and 'Should Be' so that we can compare the two and question the differences.

Now you are ready to start mapping your process.

Actually mapping your process

There is no right or wrong way to go about the actual activity of mapping a process but a common method that seems to work is the following:

1 **Get together the team who are going to do the mapping.**
This is normally the people who actually carry out the
activities and make the decisions. Depending on the scale
of the map (macro or micro), these people may all be in
the same department or they may come from across the
organization.

2 **Ensure that everyone understands the parameters of the
task** – where you are going to start, where you are going
to stop, what level of detail you want and whether you are
mapping the process 'As Is' or as 'Should Be'. (If you are
mapping 'Should Be' but you know that there is an 'As Is', it
is wise to map that as well.)

3 **Stick a roll of brown paper along the wall to map the
process on to.** Here a horizontal flow alignment normally
works best (unless you have very tall people and very high
walls!). Put up your start point symbol.

4 **Brainstorm all the activities onto large rectangular Post-
It™ notes.** Brainstorm the decisions onto square Post-Its™,
turned through 45 degrees to form diamonds.

5 **Arrange the activities along the brown paper.** Use string
and Blu-tac™ to show the flow.

*The reason for using Post-Its, string and Blu-tac is that
these will allow you to move things as you develop the map
during the mapping and improvement stages.*

6 **Check for agreement with all the people who actually
use the process or fulfil the activities.** Look for
concurrency – in any process you will usually find that
there are areas where there can be a number of sub-
processes happening at the same time and coming
together when they are all ready.

Below is a simple process map for the production of
process maps.

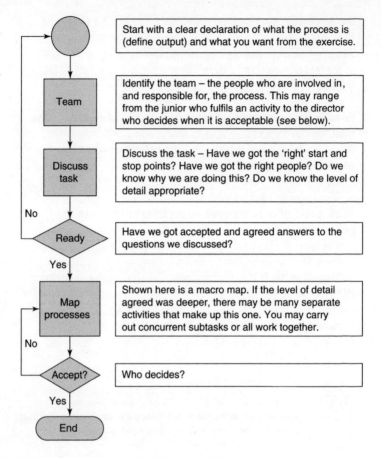

| | Start with a clear declaration of what the process is (define output) and what you want from the exercise. |

Team — Identify the team – the people who are involved in, and responsible for, the process. This may range from the junior who fulfils an activity to the director who decides when it is acceptable (see below).

Discuss task — Discuss the task – Have we got the 'right' start and stop points? Have we got the right people? Do we know why we are doing this? Do we know the level of detail appropriate?

Ready (No / Yes) — Have we got accepted and agreed answers to the questions we discussed?

Map processes — Shown here is a macro map. If the level of detail agreed was deeper, there may be many separate activities that make up this one. You may carry out concurrent subtasks or all work together.

Accept? (No / Yes) — Who decides?

End

Once you have your process mapped on the wall on brown paper, with all the activities, decisions and flows included, you are ready to actually look at analysing it for improvement opportunities. The analysis take place in three different ways, termed 'voices':

1 the voice of the process
2 the voice of the people
3 the voice of the customer.

We'll look at each of these in turn.

Analysing your process (1): The voice of the process

You need to analyse the events that make up the process in greater detail. To do this you look into:

- how long each event takes
- whether each event 'adds value'
- who carries out the events and how much effort these people expend on each event.

Combined, these produce the 'voice' of the process and the 'voice' of the people.

Time/person analysis

1 You need to annotate all activity boxes with the time it takes to fulfil each activity and who is doing it.

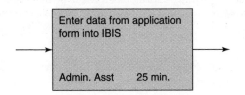

2 Then you need to annotate the arrows with the time between each activity.

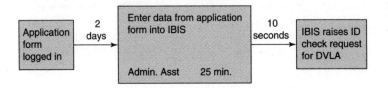

3 Once we have done this, we add all the times *inside* the activity boxes together to give us the actual process time in terms of people input.

4 Then we can do the same with all the times *between* the boxes to give us the actual process time that is non-productive.

5 Often we find that if we add up the activity times we realize that the process actually takes, say, four hours of actual working time. However, when we look at the amount of time between the boxes we find that the thing being worked on waits, or travels, for a total of several days between activities, resulting in a whole process that takes 28 days.

> ## Example
>
> A mail-order firm looked at its process from arrival of the completed order coupon to dispatch of the goods from the warehouse – the process took eight days. Out of that time only three hours was actually taken up by all the activities – stock check, financial check, order picking, packing, mailing and stock control update. The other seven days and 21 hours were spent in the internal mail or waiting in in-boxes!

Once we have annotated the times for the activities and the flow, we can now look at value analysis.

Value analysis of activities

Value analysis is a straightforward task that sounds grander than it is. It also produces some of the greatest opportunities for improvements.

Each activity in the process map should be critically assessed for 'value add'. To do this, you need to ask four questions:

1 Does the activity physically transform or transport the product-in-process in some necessary and beneficial way? If the answer is 'Yes', the activity probably adds value. (For example, if the activity adds a component to the assembly or completes/adds a piece of data.)

2 If the customer observed the activity, would he or she be happy that they were both paying for the activity and waiting while it takes place? If the answer is 'Yes', the activity probably adds value.
3 If the activity were eliminated, would the process downstream be disrupted or would the customer notice and object? If the answer is 'Yes', the activity probably adds value.
4 If the activity were eliminated, would we be breaking the law? If the answer is 'Yes', we can consider that the activity adds value. (For example, if the activity is the addition of the statutory safety notice, or the testing to a legal requirement.)

Value analysis and movement

Transport and travel *rarely* add value per se. The fact that your organization does some events in the process in one office/building/department and the next event in another requires the product to travel between steps in the process. This rarely adds value for the customer and should be reduced, avoided or worked around if possible.

Example

In a process to pay supplier invoices the invoice is authorized by the buying manager in, say, Mumbai but the accounts function is in Delhi. The accounts function will not process the authorized payment until the signed hard copy is physically in Delhi. Therefore, there is a transport issue that adds several days to the process as the document physically travels hundreds of miles. (This is also a risk factor of loss or damage en route.)

The customer may perceive a 'value of place' and be willing to pay for it. For example, a new chequebook would hold little value if it was only available at the bank's printers in Pretoria. Availability at the customer's branch in Johannesburg or by post to their home/place of work is an important part of the customer's value perception.

In order to actually assess the value add of the movement on the process map, it is useful to 'walk' the process – have a small group of people actually walk through the process as if they were the product on its journey at each stage in the process. This tends to show up:

- *the long periods that the product spends sitting in in-trays, the mail or waiting areas (the 'product' might be a patient or a litigant for some people!)*
- *the actual distance that the product, or the people processing it, travel pointlessly.*

Value analysis and decisions

We need to analyse each decision for 'value add' as well.

There are often some 'decisions' in a process map that are a form of inspection/check:

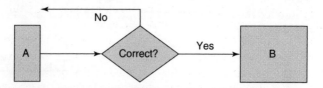

It is always worth assessing this decision for value add and looking into the reason for its existence:

- If the person who carried out activity A is the person responsible for this decision, then it isn't a separate event, and so should be removed (it is part of the activity).
- If the person who makes this decision is *not* the person who carried out activity A, we should ask *why* another person is required at this point.
- Is the person who carried out activity A unable to (be trusted to) make this decision?

Normally, we will find that the requirement for another person to make such a decision is historical; at some stage in the past the person carrying out activity A was not very proficient, a new starter for instance, and we insisted that someone else, their manager, perhaps, should check their work. They have now been doing the job for 20 years and the manager has never had to answer 'No', so we can probably say that this decision doesn't add value and can be removed from the process.

Alternately, it could be that a past manager was an autocratic control freak who didn't trust anyone and insisted on checking everything personally... If this manager is now gone, we can remove this event from the process.

Analysing Your Process (2): The Voice of the people

The 'Five + 1 Wastes'

The original concept of *Seven* + 1 Wastes originates in Toyota Lean Manufacturing and was originally described by Taiichi Ohno. The theory was that all wastes fell into one of seven categories; by recognizing these wastes, we could eliminate them and thus be as efficient as was possible.

For the purposes of process improvement (rather than getting lean), the 'Seven' have here been reduced to 'Five' – this by the simple expedient that two of the original wastes are already covered in our value analysis. The five remaining are:

1 **People overproducing** (i.e. actually making or doing more than is required)

> *For example: A member of staff spent two days plus each week producing an internal report that was disseminated to about a dozen senior managers within the organization. Owing to a major update of software, the network was going to be unavailable for 48 hours and this was going to disrupt her ability to produce this report on time one week. She contacted each of the senior managers in turn to explain that the report would be late by several days. She was aghast to discover that half of the 'customers' never saw her report; it was deleted as 'junk' every week. The other half simply filed it neatly without reading it!*

2 **People over-processing** (i.e. doing something either to a higher standard than is necessary, reinventing the wheel, or doing something a very slow way when a more effective and efficient way could easily be used).

> *For example: insisting on valeting every car that you service at your dealership even though it means that you can only service eight cars a day and therefore you lose customers; spending two hours each week producing your departmental reports in MS Word tables added up with a calculator because you don't know how to use MS Excel.*

WITH THE RIGHT MARKETING ANGLE — I MIGHT JUST HAVE SOMETHING HERE.

3 **People searching:** for things that either aren't where they should be or have run out.
4 **Unnecessary motion** by the people in the process, thus creating the situation in number 2 above.

> *Notwithstanding the example quoted earlier, we should be looking to remove any unnecessary physical movement of the people in the process for both environmental reasons and health and safety!*

5 **Defective input** (i.e. people doing something so badly it has to be done again).

There isn't much that can be said about this issue other than to suggest you look back at earlier chapters of this book!

The '+ 1' is 'not meeting the external customer requirements'. This is counted as waste since the external customer then will either:

● refuse to buy/pay for/use the output
● refuse to come back to us for more of the output, *or*
● tell other prospective customers that we have failed them, thus damaging our reputation.

This leads us into the last part of our detailed analysis, the voice of the customer.

Analysing your process (3): The voice of the customer

Every process exists because it produces something that a 'customer' wants.

The '+ 1' of our Five +1 Wastes is producing something that the customer doesn't want, predominantly because, if the customer doesn't want it, then he or she won't pay for it and you will be left with a valueless liability rather than the stock asset you created. This is obvious in the manufacturing sphere because you have shelves full of unsold goods. It is just as true, however, in the service industry because you have people doing things and being paid for it when there is no return for the organization.

The customer 'want' isn't just about your actual product though; it is also about:

● **the timing** – when your product or service is available
● **the price** – how much your product costs in relation to its perceived value
● **the place** – where your product is in relation to the customers.

An obvious signal that your process has failed in some way is going to be an adverse reaction from your customer. A complaint, grumbling, failure to buy/use your product or service, going to the competitors, quibbling over the bill, criticism, avoidance and 'cutting you out of the loop' are all bits of feedback that tell you that your process is failing.

OK, you have now mapped your process and analysed all the events in the process, looking at the wastes and the inefficiencies... Now you are ready to actually start to *improve* your processes.

Improving your processes

When you have finished all the mapping and analysis, you can actually start planning the improvement to the process. Before you plunge too deeply into this, however, it is wise to understand, and ensure everyone else does too, what you are hoping to achieve:

● Are you *expressly* looking for measurable improvements in specific areas? For example, are you looking to speed up cycle time, or reduce headcount, or lower cost, or cut carbon footprint? If so, by how much?
● Are you simply looking to check that your process is as efficient as it can be?
● Are you looking to find ways to help your staff achieve more in the same period of time?
● Are you actually just tacking 'improvement' on to mapping, which you are doing in order to generate the documentation needed for a quality system?

- Are you looking to improve capability in order to take on new work and increase profitability/stability (rather than be able to reduce headcount)?

It is valuable to ensure that the same people who did all the work to date are as heavily involved in the improvement stage; they know the processes, have done all the analysis and therefore will be better able to see the reasons for keeping certain events in the process. Also, they are the people who will make the new process work; you want them to have both ownership and responsibility for the new processes actually functioning so that you don't immediately go into a situation where you have a gulf between 'As Is' and 'Should Be'!

It is best to start with your 'As Is' process laid out graphically in front of the team with all the 'data' from the analysis. Next:

- Look at the overall process and ask yourself the question 'Is it OK?' It may be that the answer is either 'Yes' or 'Pretty much, with a few tweaks'. If the answer was 'Yes', then (depending on your overall objective) you may want to LEAVE IT ALONE – 'if it ain't broke, don't fix it'. Many managers have dug themselves into a hole by trying to change things for the sake of it. If the answer was 'Pretty much, with a few tweaks', then make the tweaks. Use as rational an approach as you did to the analysis; consider the time things take and the value they add.
- If there are *major* areas that need to be changed, then you may want to start off with the question 'Is it worth *us* changing the process or should we just outsource it?'
- If you are going to undertake improvements to the process, then make sure that you map the improved process so that everyone can see the differences and they become a formal part of your SOPs. Consider small and radical changes to events within the process: ways in which an activity can be improved *slightly*, such as improved timing, material or method; or ways in which the activity can be removed altogether or reduced dramatically.

Summary

Today you have learned that pretty much everyone uses processes and that processes can be mapped, analysed and improved. You have learned how to map processes and to tell the difference between a process as it should be and a process as it actually is. You have also learned how to manage a team to map the process with you to get the benefit of their input and expertise.

You have learned how to analyse the efficiency and effectiveness of a process, looking at the process time, the waiting and travelling time, and the value of different events in the process. You have learned about the Five + 1 wastes, and how they can cause a process to fail. Again, you have learned how to manage a team to carry out these tasks.

Finally, you have learned how to manage the improvement of a process, giving your people the ability to input to making their own lives easier or more productive.

In the German language there is a word, *Schlimmbesserung*, which refers to the act of making something worse in the attempt to improve it. Armed with what you have learned today you should now be able to avoid this!

Tomorrow we will look at how to improve your team management skills, by using the 'seven Cs of team building'.

SUNDAY

MONDAY

TUESDAY

WEDNESDAY

THURSDAY

FRIDAY

SATURDAY

Fact-check (answers at back)

1. 'Mapping' your process allows you to...
   a) Explain it easily to people new to the process ❏
   b) Assess your process for bottlenecks and critical paths ❏
   c) Measure and improve time and resource usage ❏
   d) All of the above ❏

2. The start point of a process in a process map is usually denoted by a...
   a) Rectangle ❏
   b) Arrow ❏
   c) Circle ❏
   d) Ellipse ❏

3. Every decision should be shown as a question to which the answer should be...
   a) Yes ❏
   b) No ❏
   c) Maybe ❏
   d) Yes or no ❏

4. To make it easier to follow on a PC screen, many people map their processes...
   a) Left to right ❏
   b) Top to bottom ❏
   c) Right to left ❏
   d) In binary code ❏

5. There is no need to show a decision that is a quality check as a separate event if...
   a) The person who carried out the activity is responsible for the quality check themselves ❏
   b) A manager is responsible for the quality check ❏
   c) The manager can't usually be bothered to carry out the quality check ❏
   d) Quality isn't important ❏

6. When analysing time on a process map, you look at the time it takes to actually carry out each activity and what other time?
   a) People's break times ❏
   b) The time between the activities and decisions ❏
   c) The shelf life of the product ❏
   d) How much time could be saved if people worked harder ❏

7. Several different activities that take place at the same time are referred to as...
   a) Concurrent ❏
   b) Converting ❏
   c) Concretions ❏
   d) Concertos ❏

8. There are four criteria for defining whether an event adds value. Which of the following is not a real criterion?
a) The event physically transforms or transports the product-in-process in some necessary and beneficial way. ❏
b) If the customer observed the activity, he or she would be happy that they were both paying for the activity and waiting while it takes place. ❏
c) If the activity were eliminated, the process downstream would be disrupted or the customer would notice and object. ❏
d) If the activity were eliminated, we would save time and money and therefore make our life easier. ❏

9. If you improve a process, you should map the new improved process so that...
a) The new process becomes part of the SOPs and can be explained to people easily ❏
b) Everyone can see that you are a great improver ❏
c) If it goes wrong, you'll know who suggested the change and can blame them ❏
d) You can write a paper to publicize your brilliance ❏

10. *Schlimmbesserung* means...
a) Improving processes ❏
b) Throwing out inefficient processes ❏
c) Trying to make it better but actually making things worse ❏
d) Changing nothing because this is the way things have always been done ❏

FRIDAY

Improve your teamwork

Now that you are a manager, your personal future is inextricably linked to the success of your team:

- If your team fails in its objectives, you will fail in yours.
- If your team falls apart, and they all leave the organization, your job will become harder as you struggle to recruit new people and train them.
- If your team complains about you to your boss, you will get a poor annual review.
- If your team complains about you to everybody else, you won't be able to recruit, and you'll look bad in the eyes of your peers.

A team functions by 'synergy': your team isn't just a group of individuals each doing their own thing in isolation; it is a group bonded by a common goal who support each other to produce a greater output than they could alone.

If you put a dozen people together in a situation, and they all want the same outcome, they will probably, eventually, meld into a team. Do you want to wait until 'eventually' and rely on 'probably'? If you do, you won't become a better manager in a week!

You need to make a concerted effort to create, build and nurture a team.

Here is how...

The 'Seven Cs of team building'

There are seven 'areas' that you need to *consciously* and *consistently* work on in order to manage an effective team. The title of each area starts with the letter C.

Commitment to objectives

Each person has to be wholeheartedly committed to the overall objectives of the team. This has several implications for you as a manager:

- You have to have clearly communicated the **overall objective of the team** to each and every person – not just once, but sufficiently regularly to remind everyone why they are here. The frequency with which you have to do this will change according to the situation and people's reactions to it: sometimes in moments of great pressure it is necessary to reiterate the point of the team's effort; similarly sometimes when everything is easy it is vital to remind people of the need for their effort.
- You have to agree **individual objectives** that clearly contribute to the overall team objective; when people believe that they can achieve these objectives they will be committed to them.
- You may constantly have to remind some people just how important *their* achievement of *their* objectives is in **the bigger scheme of things**; the hotel manager's job is important and the chef's is obviously vital, but so are the chambermaid's and the bellhop's.
- You need to ensure that people are **aware of the progress** they are achieving towards those objectives. When people can see that they are making progress, this in itself increases their commitment and motivation.
- You need to help people to **achieve** these objectives. That means that you provide them with the information, the tools and resources, the protection and the peace to get on and do the job that you have given them.

Coordination

A better manager coordinates the team effectively, ensuring:

- that no one is duplicating the work of another, as this is wasteful and annoys people
- that there are no gaps between the roles of the team members, preventing things from metaphorically falling though the holes in the team and getting missed
- that everyone knows what everyone else does and is doing; this not only makes people feel part of a greater organism but also helps everyone to value everyone else's contribution
- that resources are allocated equitably
- an 'internal customer' attitude exists between the team members; each values the contribution and the needs of the others leading to reliability.

Communication

Though we've looked at this in detail on Tuesday, let's recap what was said there in the context of the team. The better manager:

- makes sure that there is effective feedback within the team – from the manager to team members, from team members back to the manager, and between team members
- ensures that the team is kept informed of what is happening today in the organization and what is expected to happen in the future
- communicates with everyone on a fair footing, making sure that no one is left out or 'kept in the dark' about things that affect them
- works hard to prevent information overload for the team, where important messages are missed due to the sheer quantity of 'chatter'
- passes team opinions up the chain of command where appropriate so that the team see that their opinions count with the more senior people with whom they may have little contact.

Culture of collaboration or competition?

Depending on the type of activity you and your team undertake, a better manager fosters an appropriate culture:

- In some circumstances, it is appropriate to foster a culture of *gentle* competition between team members. This may

be applicable for example, in a sales context, where sales people can be encouraged to compare their individual performance against their colleagues'.

- Any form of competition is based around the setting of an objective; you set out to achieve a goal relative to either a fixed point (e.g. to beat the world record, or to beat your 'personal best') or a moving target (e.g. to beat another team, person or even everyone).
- However, although a spirit of *internal* competition can provide short-term interest and motivation, it is seldom appropriate for a manager to set his or her team to compete with each other permanently – especially if you award a valuable 'prize' to the winning person or people. Every time you announce winners, you are also announcing losers.
- When a manager sets the team up to thrash the competition, they start working in collaboration with each other against a common 'foe'. This spirit of collaboration is highly conducive to teamwork, so long as people have meaningful objectives within the overall goal.

Appropriate goals in this last instance may be:

✓ to beat the opposition in an absolute way (i.e. through a greater number of sales or higher value of sales)
✓ to increase market share
✓ to 'steal' the opposition's customers.

Alternatively, the team may operate in competition against themselves, trying to improve on last month's figures or those of the same period last year. They may be encouraged to compete against the clock, increasing their output in a given period or reducing cycle time for their outputs. While it is clearly quite easy to manage this in a sales setting, where the numbers are easy to come by, it is also possible to effectively manage it in non-sales areas – e.g. through:

✓ improved customer satisfaction reports
✓ reduced complaints
✓ higher customer loyalty.

Control

Many inexperienced or ineffective managers fall into the trap of presuming that they have to be in control of everything that happens in their team. This is a huge mistake, and it leads to some major problems for team managers and their team members alike.

'I'm the manager so I must control everything that happens in my team'	
Problems this creates for the manager	Problems this creates for the team members
• You HAVE to make all decisions; therefore you are going to be constantly inundated by people with questions	• People never learn to become independent; they learn only to ask you every time
• If you aren't there, nothing gets done; you can't afford to take a break	• People resent their dependence and feel stifled
• You have to have a constant stream of new solutions to problems	• People never develop the ability to try out a solution; they begin to believe that their own ideas would work, simply because they never get tested
• You have to have answers immediately	• People become lazy and reliant because you made them that way!
• When it doesn't work, it is YOUR fault	• People have no ownership of the solution – that is your job; consequently, they have little motivation to make your solution work

A better manager does not feel the need to control everything with a vicelike grip; he or she is prepared to empower people, to give them the right to make decisions for themselves.

If this sounds like a recipe for anarchy, consider this little fable:

Case study

The Board of Directors at a hotel chain were concerned at the increasing cost of goodwill payments being made to customers with complaints. Their discussions highlighted that they were making comparatively large goodwill payments for comparatively small complaints, and they noticed that the time lapse between the initial complaint and the final settlement was getting longer. This delay was causing the customers to become more and more demanding.

The Board were discussing the matter at a meeting. One of the directors heard the boardroom waitress mutter something under her breath and asked her to share her comment. She was reluctant to do so but eventually, after being promised that no ill would come of it, she said, 'If you just trusted the front-line staff to offer an immediate solution, the problems would almost all go away.'

She was asked to give an example, so she chose one that the Board had been discussing: a customer had sent his shirt to be washed at the hotel laundry, the shirt was returned with a scorch mark, the customer had had to go and buy a new shirt, and had consequently been late for a business meeting. The meeting had gone badly and the customer felt that his lateness was at least partly to blame. After complaining to the concierge and then being passed to the duty manager, he had become quite demanding and the matter was escalated to the hotel manager and then up to the chain's regional manager. Eventually, when the matter was four months old, a settlement was made by the regional director for several hundred dollars. The waitress went on to give her solution. If the chambermaid had been able to go to the customer, apologize and take the customer straight to the local department store and buy him a replacement shirt, the problem would have been solved in a matter of hours for the cost of a shirt.

The director, having listened to her suggestion immediately proposed that all staff should be empowered to spend up to $25 to fix a customer's problem on the spot. The Finance Director was appalled; the chain employed 7,000 staff and at $25 per head the potential loss was $175,000 a day!

The Board, however, decided to trial the proposal.

Customer satisfaction went up and goodwill spend came down.

So a better manager gives trust to the individuals in the team, but sets clear parameters within which people can be confident that their judgement is allowed.

Creativity and challenge

A better manager encourages his or her team to be creative. No, we aren't suggesting that they be encouraged to sing their sales pitch or act out their role in modern dance. But a better manager expects team members to *think*, to use their imagination, and to pursue ideas.

A better manager will:

- ask people their opinions and then listen to them – not just 'gossip'-type opinions, but serious work-type opinions
- encourage people to make suggestions for ways to improve, not just their own day-to-day job, but also those of their colleagues and co-workers
- get the team together for suggestions and ideas – to build on each other's ideas and to critique each other's ideas
- encourage their team members to stretch themselves with activities that may be outside their normal jobs, such as taking a junior under their wing; acting as a work shadow for someone from another department; giving a tour to a school

party, or writing a piece for the organization's newsletter or the trade press
- identify and nurture potential – putting people forward for promotions and opportunities, even if it means that they might lose them from their team.

Consequences

A better manager aims to develop his or her team to maturity. A prime indicator of maturity in human beings, as we saw in the Introduction, is the capacity to identify and accept the consequences of actions and inactions. So a better manager will help the team to recognize that there are consequences to all that they do and all that they should do but fail to do. This means that a better manager will:

- give credit where credit is due;
- ensure that there is appropriate reward or recognition for effort, for success and for achievement. This is not solely the achievement of formal targets and objectives but also the provision of support to teammates, activity and actions above and beyond the call of duty and the use of initiative;
- recognize when someone is 'coasting' and doing the bare minimum to keep out of trouble... and addressing this before it becomes a habit or a problem;
- 'manage' someone whose performance is poor, including identifying the real reason behind poor performance and providing an effective response. Where an individual lacks skill,

the better manager provides the opportunity to develop that skill. Where an individual lacks motivation, the better manager takes action to provide that motivation. That action may be the promise of a reward for achievement or the promise of a punishment for continued failure to achieve. While this is clearly a strong aspect of personal performance management it is also critical to good teamwork; team members who feel that a manager is making them carry people who are not performing will resent both the underperforming team member and their underperforming manager.

Managing 'remote' or 'virtual' teams

As the world becomes metaphorically smaller and we all spend more of our time working cross-border, more of us find ourselves managing teams that are spread across the globe. Even if you are not working for a global organization, the likelihood is that you may be running a team of people who are based in differing departments of your organization. This form of 'matrix management' is commonplace for project teams and is also becoming more popular for service delivery. Luckily, we are no longer reliant on the steam-packet postal service or even the Morse code telegraph. Here is a list of 10 top tips for managing virtual, or remote, teams:

1 **Get to know virtual team members before** you form a team. This allows you to understand what the team dynamics might be when you put together a team.
2 Have your team members **generate ideas** on how they would like to communicate better with each other. Not everyone likes the same style and, if you dictate things, it may be detrimental.
3 Launch your regular team conference calls with some **light-hearted chat** – ask questions rather than talking yourself.
4 Be sensitive to **different time zones** when holding virtual meetings so that the same person does not always have to attend late at night. Rotate the calls to differing times

throughout the year. Be sensitive also to people's 'other boss' if you are managing a part-time team in a matrix management organization.

5 Use conference calls or online meeting rooms to discuss problems and **ask the entire team for suggestions.** Ask people who are in different geographic areas how they solve the problems. This helps to build team spirit and allows team members to get to know each other.

6 Establish an **online forum** that you don't manage. You will find that people will become empowered and share ideas.

7 Have the **whole team welcome new members** and introduce themselves, either at a virtual team meeting or one-to-one.

8 Hold a **quarterly team meeting** (using webinar video conferencing) *just* for **team-building activities.** Consider a 'theme', such as having everyone dress in Hawaiian shirts or decorate their background scene in a particular way. Try a virtual 'happy hour', where no direct work is allowed and just conversation.

9 Hold a real **face-to-face get-together** (if fiscally possible) for the whole team once a year. At this event, take advantage of team building and bonding opportunities.

10 **Be very direct when managing conflict.** If two people or groups are on either side of an issue, make sure they speak with each other directly, preferably face to face or, if that's not possible, by video phone or VOIP video call. This allows a better chance of people picking up on non-verbal cues.

Summary

Today you have seen that, although teams do form by evolution, there are lots of things you can do to create a team ethos much more quickly. You have also seen that leading a team is better and easier than having to monitor and supervise a gang of individuals. You have learned the 'Seven Cs of team building' and seen that a better manager is not necessarily one who is in total control of every tiny detail of what is happening in his or her team. In fact, the better manager is the one who encourages team members to share the responsibility as well as the accountability for the success of individuals and of the team as a whole. This sharing of the burden presents short and long-term benefits to the team members, as well as making your life easier.

You have also learned that teams can function in a decentralized way, scattered across departments, different buildings or even different continents. You have been introduced to day-to-day methods to help this to work more effectively.

Tomorrow we will look at how, as a manager, you can make work enjoyable – both for your team and for you.

SUNDAY

MONDAY

TUESDAY

WEDNESDAY

THURSDAY

FRIDAY

SATURDAY

Fact-check (answers at back)

1. Why is your personal future bound up with the success of your team?
a) If your team fails in its objectives, you will fail in yours ❏
b) If your team falls apart, and they all leave the organization, your job will become harder as you struggle to recruit new people and train them ❏
c) If your team complains about you to your boss, you will get a poor annual review ❏
d) All of the above ❏

2. The 'Seven Cs' are:
a) Commitment, Control, Culture, Communication, Coordination, Creativity and Consequences ❏
b) Commitment, Coercion, Control, Communication, Creativity and Consequences ❏
c) Commitment, Command, Control, Coercion, Competition, Creativity and Communication ❏
d) Compulsion, Coercion, Command, Contact, Cruelty and Cost ❏

3. People within the team have to take responsibility for the consequences of their actions or inactions. This is because...
a) It allows you to blame them if they let you down ❏
b) It is a clear indicator of their maturity ❏
c) It makes your life easier ❏
d) You had to take responsibility when you were in their place so they must now ❏

4. If, as a manager, you insist on being in total control of everything, you run the risk of...
a) Having to be the solver of all problems ❏
b) Constantly being distracted by your people coming to you to ask your permission ❏
c) People not buying in to solutions and new processes ❏
d) All of the above ❏

5. When running a remote, or virtual, team, who should introduce themselves to a new member?
a) You as the team leader ❏
b) Every member of the virtual team ❏
c) The people geographically closest to the new person ❏
d) The people who will work most with the new person ❏

6. When you hold conference or video conference calls with a virtual team that is global you should...
a) Always hold calls at the same time of day to establish a pattern ❏
b) Move call times around the working week to avoid establishing a boring routine ❏
c) Be considerate of people who may be in different time zones and make sure that calls aren't always making the same people work out of hours ❏
d) Make calls with little or no notice to 'keep people on their toes' ❏

7. If you don't manage poor performance in one team member, the effect this will have on the other members of the team is that...
a) They will lose respect for you as they have to carry the poor performer ❑
b) They will start to believe that you set low standards, so their performance may fall as well ❑
c) Both a) and b) ❑
d) They will see you as a nice person and will respect you more for this ❑

8. A better manager will put forward people for promotion in order to...
a) Recognize and reward a person's potential ❑
b) Get rid of a poor performer ❑
c) Get rid of a troublemaker ❑
d) Remove someone who is so good that they threaten the better manager's own job security ❑

9. Empowering team members is likely to result in...
a) People taking responsibility for their own quality ❑
b) People taking advantage of you ❑
c) Faster resolution of problems and issues ❑
d) a) and c) ❑

10. A better manager not only gives feedback to the team and its members, but also...
a) Seeks feedback from the team ❑
b) Avoids situations where team members can give feedback ❑
c) Actively discourages feedback from team members as it is 'criticism of the manager' ❑
d) Passes on feedback from outside the team without any investigation of whether that feedback is justified or fair ❑

SATURDAY

Provide enjoyment

The traditional work ethic suggests that everyone's day should have: 'Eight hours work, eight hours leisure and eight hours of rest.' The implication is that 'work' is not meant to be enjoyable. It is meant to be hard and miserable to provide a foil against leisure time. Why? People spend most of the day, on most days of the week, at work and working – why should it be an unpleasant activity?

Repeated studies suggest that, in the modern world, employees who are 'happy' are significantly more productive than employees who are miserable. Of course, it isn't your job to make people 'happy'; only the individual can make the decision to be happy or miserable. As a manager, however, you have the opportunity to try to make an environment where people are *able to be* 'happy'. This doesn't only benefit them; it benefits you as well, not only in the realms of their productivity, but also in the way this makes your job easier.

We aren't talking here about providing desk toys or pool tables at the workplace. We are talking about things that you can do for no financial cost.

What do we mean by 'enjoyment?'

- **People generally enjoy feeling as if they are achieving something.** In order to achieve something, you have to know what the something is that you are trying to achieve, so clear and unambiguous objectives are a fundamental element of giving people a feeling of achievement. We looked at this in detail on Monday where we focused on the business point of setting objectives.

- **People enjoy it when their efforts are recognized.** If you work hard at something, for someone, but no one seems to notice, you rapidly lose the will to work. So recognizing, and rewarding, effort and results is a manager's way of keeping people motivated.

- **People generally enjoy having a challenge to rise to.** While it may seem that happiness lies in an easy life, reality suggests that this often results in listlessness and misery. You have only to look at the examples of people who inherit large amounts of money to see that having it *too* easy can lead to a life without meaning. This does not mean, however, that you should *simply* keep raising the targets; that is usually interpreted as evidence that you are taking your staff for granted! The provision of new, stimulating and challenging work is a major differentiator between a better manager and a slave-driver. Taking someone outside their 'comfort zone', in a controlled and safe way, is an excellent way to provide people with a challenge and opportunity to grow.

- **People enjoy being 'listened' to.** If someone has a suggestion or an idea, or if they have a complaint or a problem, then listen to them. Listen carefully and comprehensively. Ask them questions until you have a full understanding of the issue. Then, and only then, decide what you are going to do about it. Tell them what you are going to do about it, and tell them why. It is perfectly correct, in some instances, to *decide* that you are going to do nothing. However, if you don't explain why, it may look as if you have simply ignored the person.

What is the outcome of all this enjoyment?

Employees are not the only people to benefit from enjoying their work; there are distinct advantages for you, as the manager, as well.

When people enjoy their work, and respect, or even like, their boss, they are...

Staff/Team members' reactions:	Which means for the manager:
• ...Less likely to take time off sick	• Less wasted time managing temporary staff and return-to-work interviews
• ...More likely to *want* to achieve results	• Less need for you to monitor timekeeping, quality and output
• ...Less likely to leave	• Less wasted time recruiting replacements • Less risk of getting the wrong replacement • Less time training replacements
• ...More likely to show initiative	• Less time fire-fighting, managing crises and having to solve other people's problems
• ...Less likely to criticize you or the organization	• Less worry about what is going on behind your back • Fewer unpleasant surprises
• ...More likely to be flexible when things have to be done that are not 'by the book'	• Faster and easier response to ad hoc management issues
• ...Less likely to have serious disagreements with their peers	• Less need for you to arbitrate in arguments

The benefits don't stop there either: your team's customers, be they internal or external, will also benefit from these things. Staff or team members are...

Staff/Team members' reactions:	Which means for the customer:
• ...Less likely to take time off sick	• Better continuity of contact
• ...More likely to *want* to achieve results	• More likely to get results
• ...Are less likely to leave	• Better continuity of contact and continued service
• ...More likely to show initiative	• Quicker response to special requests or problems
• ...Less likely to criticize you or the organization	• Dealing with happy people is generally more pleasant than working with a misery!
• ...More likely to be flexible when things have to be done that are not 'by the book'	• Quicker response and probably better outcomes to special requests and problems
• Less likely to have serious disagreements with their peers	• Dealing with happy people is generally more pleasant than working with a misery!

> **'Good customer service is giving the customer what he expects. Great customer service is looking as if you are enjoying giving the customer what he expects.'**
>
> Gordon Bessant, founder of AMT

10 ways to improve workplace enjoyment

1 Keep things as informal and natural as you can. Avoid closed doors and private offices, have stand-up meetings rather than formal sitting-round-the-board-table meetings.
2 Allow people to decorate their personal workspace according to their own taste (obviously within reason and decency).

3 Wherever possible, rotate routine tasks that the team fulfils. For instance, if you have a regular report to produce, try getting a different person to produce it each month. This may seem to be making unnecessary work, but it a) provides opportunities to people to learn new skills, b) ensures that boring routine tasks don't always fall to the same person, c) allows people to discuss with each other the best way to do things.

4 Delegate the *interesting* and *exciting* tasks that come in; pick different people to do these tasks, rather than always going for the same person. This way the task becomes a reward in itself. You can even put these tasks on open offer and see who *wants* to take them on.

5 Encourage people to 'chat' – not necessarily gossip but light discussions at the coffee machine or water-cooler.

Case study

At the London HQ of a global company, it was noticed that people were so busy at their desks that the office was virtually silent. No one wanted to be the only person to break the silence, so the culture became one where people had their heads down over their screens and whispered into their phones. The company took two actions to break this uncomfortable habit; they actually piped background 'noise' (not music but actual office noise) into the offices! They made a rule that you couldn't drink or eat at your desk but only in designated 'lounges' where they put soft chairs and bar stools and the coffee machines and water coolers. This got people to go to these areas, and meet and chat with other employees from different teams.

6 Delegate the *difficult* and the *challenging* tasks that crop up; pick different people to do these tasks, rather than always going for your best trouble-shooter. This way the task becomes a chance for people to show (to you and themselves) what they are capable of. You can even put these tasks on open offer and see who *doesn't want* to take them on.

7 Engage in 'Planned Spontaneous Recognition'. Decide on something little that you want to reward someone, or the whole team, for. Get a token reward – a box of doughnuts, a bar of chocolate, a desk toy, for instance. Catch the person/people doing what you want to reward them for, and give them the reward with a word of *personal* thanks. (Note: this isn't from the organization; it is from you.)

8 Look for opportunities to develop your people. This does not *only* mean sending them on training courses, but in the same way that points 3, 4 and 6 above all help people to develop new skills, try to find other ways as well. Give people self-help books to read and report on to the team, or task people to investigate new thinking in your business area. Get people to liaise with other parts of the organization about what your team does.

9 Look for opportunities to get the team together informally. For example, have a team lunch occasionally, give people some notice and get some appropriate food in, or ask everyone to bring in their own and have an in-office picnic. Encourage socializing and non-work discussion. Get people talking about their home lives, their hobbies, and their families. (Try to avoid having these social events out of hours, as that may well exclude people who have other commitments in their life.)

10 'Manage the Grinch'... Virtually every workplace has a Grinch; a miserable person who moans about everything and anything and who is only happy when they are complaining.

This person sucks the joy out of enthusiastic new starters, belittles any suggestion made by their co-workers as being pointless because 'they' won't listen, and makes your life difficult by opposing everything you try to do (either overtly or behind your back). Try hard to get them to be positive, repeatedly attempt to get them to see the bright side of things and to contribute in a happy and helpful way. Do this if only for the sake of their own health; studies suggest that, generally, happy people live longer! If, after all your efforts, they simply won't lighten up then manage them out of the organization; sack them, downsize them, make them redundant or retire them.

Summary

Today we have addressed the fact that work shouldn't be a miserable activity, not for you and not for the people you manage. You have learned why enjoyment in the workplace is beneficial and how it benefits the team, you as the manager, and the team's customers.

Please note that you haven't been advised to engage in any silliness! Workplace enjoyment isn't about practical jokes and pranks, and it isn't about allowing people to spend their day surfing the Net or playing pinball in the office. It isn't about wearing silly hats. It isn't about taking everyone to Disneyland. Neither is it about giving people enormous salaries or bonuses.

Enjoyment is about people feeling engaged, about them feeling valued as human beings not just human *resources*. Enjoyment is about knowing your colleagues and valuing them. It is about variety and challenge, developing and growing.

Fact-check (answers at the back)

1. When people enjoy their work they are...
a) More likely to take time off sick ❑
b) Less likely to take time off sick ❑
c) Will probably take the same amount of time off sick ❑
d) Wouldn't dare to take time off sick ❑

2. If someone has a suggestion you should...
a) Make time to listen to their idea, fully understand it and then decide what to do ❑
b) Send them to the Research and Development Department ❑
c) Tell them that it isn't their job to think of suggestions ❑
d) Take their suggestion as a criticism of your management ❑

3. If someone has a complaint or a grievance you should...
a) Tell them that they are the office Grinch and sack them ❑
b) Listen to them, understand their complaint and then decide what to do about it ❑
c) Ignore it and hope they will not bring it up again ❑
d) Send them to the Human Resources Department ❑

4. Making sure that people enjoy their work means that as a manager you should...
a) Let people do what they want to do at work ❑
b) Not challenge people to step outside their comfort zone ❑
c) Not ask people to do things that they aren't already good at ❑
d) None of the above ❑

5. Getting the team together for a social event is best done...
a) In the evening after work ❑
b) In the morning before work ❑
c) During the working day ❑
d) At the weekend ❑

6. Rotating routine tasks between team members helps because it...
a) Keeps people wondering what they are going to be asked to do next ❑
b) Spreads the blame if something goes wrong ❑
c) Makes sure no one gets the boring work all the time ❑
d) Looks as if you are actually managing rather than leaving things alone ❑

7. The best way to ensure people have fun at work is to...
a) Have a fancy-dress day once a month ❏
b) Go out for a meal each month and get drunk together ❏
c) Give an 'employee of the month' award and have it presented by someone dressed as a well-known cartoon character ❏
d) None of the above ❏

8. If you have a Grinch in your team you should...
a) Recommend them for a job in another team or department ❏
b) Accept that there is nothing you can do to change their behaviour – it's 'just the way they are' – and put up with it ❏
c) Attempt to get them to lighten up, and if they won't, manage them out of the organization ❏
d) Recognize that they are right, admit that the organization is run by idiots, and join them in their cynical misery ❏

9. Delegating the difficult and challenging jobs is a good idea because it...
a) Allows you to get your own back on someone who has annoyed you ❏
b) Sets up someone else to blame when it all goes wrong ❏
c) Gives you more time to enjoy the rewards of having been made the manager ❏
d) Gives the person the chance to prove what they can do ❏

10. Staff enjoying their work offers a benefit to customers because...
a) Dealing with happy people is generally more pleasant than working with a misery ❏
b) The customer is always right and happy people are less likely to argue ❏
c) Customers are less likely to complain to a happy person ❏
d) There is no benefit to customers; it only benefits the manager ❏

Surviving in tough times

The seven days represented in each chapter relate to how to be a better manager. It doesn't make a lot of difference whether you want to be a better manager when times are good and things are easy, or when the times are tough and only the strong survive. Being a better manager is appropriate in either case.

The difference is that human nature says that when times are tough there is an increase in the blame culture and a tendency to batten down the hatches and just try to weather the storm. However, it is even more important not to lose sight of the things that make a better manager. Here is a brief 10-point guide to keep you on the road to success even when everything seems to be falling down around you.

1 Manage the crises – don't let the crisis manage you

Keep a cool head; don't overreact or react in haste. Before you act, stop and think:

1 Remind yourself what the objective is.
2 Ask if it is still a viable objective: if it is, stick with it; if it isn't, change it!

3 Look at what is going wrong, identify the barriers and look at ways to overcome or circumvent them.

Avoid 'organizational procrastination' – there may never be a 'right time' to act, so after you have carried out the above, get on and do it!

2 Smile, smile, smile

No matter how great the crisis, or how tough the market, being miserable won't help. A positive mental attitude may, on the other hand, make the difference...

- between your people following you and people letting you walk alone
- between customers buying from you or going to your competitors
- between your boss or your shareholders investing in you or withholding funds.

We aren't talking here about mindless optimism and a refusal to accept the facts, but a genuine personal belief.

3 Deal with the negative people

The Grinches really come to the fore when times are tough. They prevent you from being positive and they suck all the energy from everyone else. Do not leave them to infect everyone with their negative attitude. Manage them *in* by getting them to focus on the positives that there are rather than the negatives. Keep them busy and ask their opinions about the possible solutions. Or manage them *out*.

4 Motivate people when all seems lost

Better managers...

- set an example to their people
- keep the faith and are very visible

- remain calm and positive
- don't cut everything to the bare essentials
- focus on the people and the possibilities, not the problems and the pitfalls.

Better managers rise under pressure when less able managers get swamped in the general malaise.

5 Trust your team

When the going gets tough, a poor manager starts to micro-manage; without trust in the team, he or she must make every decision and control every little aspect of the job. The poor manager demands hourly progress reports that simply slow the job down and which make people feel useless. A better manager gets the team more involved, not less. He or she asks people's opinions and for their input to solutions. A better manager encourages and allows people to show and use their initiative. A better manager recognizes that the people don't want it all to fail any more than he or she does, so the better manager lets people get on with their job.

6 Think outside the box

Yes, it *is* a very overused phrase, 'think outside the box'. However, a better manager had better do so. There is a definition of madness that says that 'madness is expecting a different result when you do the same thing you have always done'. So, as a manager, you have to try something different; have a brainstorm of the '5 Ms' that are used in cause and effect analysis – Manpower, Method, Management, Material, Machinery. If you changed any one of them, could it increase the likelihood of success?

7 Learn from the successes of others

Although you do need to think outside the box, don't try to reinvent the wheel. If another organization has found a way out of the doldrums, then look at its solution and see if it would work for you. Do not *just* copy it slavishly; not every successful method translates between geographies, market sectors or customer bases, so have a good think before you commit.

8 Focus on cutting unnecessary costs

The key to success here is the definition of *unnecessary*. It is vital to remember that if you cut the marketing budget today there will probably be less in the income pipeline tomorrow. If you cut staff training this year, your staff will be behind next year. So, if you are going to cut costs, look at the capacity for production in the future, rather than just the return you get on those costs today.

9 Plan for the future

There will be one, and it will probably be better than you envisage, so have a goal and a plan. Don't get caught in that procrastination mentioned in point 1 above. Keep behaving as if there will be a future; if you start giving the impression that you don't believe in the future, you will have a heck of a job convincing anyone else to believe in one. Think of the analogy of a person overboard from a ship in mid-ocean: the only reasons to 'keep your head above the water' is because you believe that you might get swept ashore or rescued, and if you don't have that belief...

10 Be cruel to be kind

The harsh reality of life is that you may at some stage be faced with a 'devil's alternative'. You may have to be prepared to make someone redundant for the overall greater good. It isn't easy to pick one person to sacrifice (metaphorically) in order to be able to keep the rest of the team going, but, hey, no one ever said that being a better manager was going to be an easy job!

Answers

Sunday: 1b; 2b; 3a; 4c; 5a; 6a; 7a; 8c; 9b; 10a.

Monday: 1b; 2d; 3c; 4a; 5d; 6b; 7d; 8c; 9a; 10a.

Tuesday: 1d; 2a; 3c; 4a; 5c; 6a; 7d; 8c; 9a; 10a.

Wednesday: 1b; 2a; 3c; 4c; 5b; 6c; 7d; 8a; 9d; 10b.

Thursday: 1d; 2c; 3d; 4b; 5a; 6b; 7a; 8d; 9a; 10c.

Friday: 1d; 2a; 3b; 4d; 5b; 6c; 7c; 8a; 9d; 10a.

Saturday: 1b; 2a; 3b; 4d; 5c; 6c; 7d; 8c; 9d; 10a.

ALSO AVAILABLE IN THE 'IN A WEEK' SERIES

BODY LANGUAGE FOR MANAGEMENT ● BOOKKEEPING AND ACCOUNTING ● CUSTOMER CARE ● DEALING WITH DIFFICULT PEOPLE ● EMOTIONAL INTELLIGENCE ● FINANCE FOR NON-FINANCIAL MANAGERS ● INTRODUCING MANAGEMENT ● MANAGING YOUR BOSS ● MARKET RESEARCH ● NEURO-LINGUISTIC PROGRAMMING ● OUTSTANDING CREATIVITY ● PLANNING YOUR CAREER ● SPEED READING ● SUCCEEDING AT INTERVIEWS ● SUCCESSFUL APPRAISALS ● SUCCESSFUL ASSERTIVENESS ● SUCCESSFUL BUSINESS PLANS ● SUCCESSFUL CHANGE MANAGEMENT ● SUCCESSFUL COACHING ● SUCCESSFUL COPYWRITING ● SUCCESSFUL CVS ● SUCCESSFUL INTERVIEWING

For information about other titles in the series, please visit www.inaweek.co.uk

ALSO AVAILABLE IN THE 'IN A WEEK' SERIES

SUCCESSFUL JOB APPLICATIONS ● SUCCESSFUL JOB HUNTING ● SUCCESSFUL KEY ACCOUNT MANAGEMENT ● SUCCESSFUL LEADERSHIP ● SUCCESSFUL MARKETING ● SUCCESSFUL MARKETING PLANS ● SUCCESSFUL MEETINGS ● SUCCESSFUL MEMORY TECHNIQUES ● SUCCESSFUL MENTORING ● SUCCESSFUL NEGOTIATING ● SUCCESSFUL NETWORKING ● SUCCESSFUL PEOPLE SKILLS ● SUCCESSFUL PRESENTING ● SUCCESSFUL PROJECT MANAGEMENT ● SUCCESSFUL PSYCHOMETRIC TESTING ● SUCCESSFUL PUBLIC RELATIONS ● SUCCESSFUL RECRUITMENT ● SUCCESSFUL SELLING ● SUCCESSFUL STRATEGY ● SUCCESSFUL TIME MANAGEMENT ● TACKLING INTERVIEW QUESTIONS

For information about other titles in the series, please visit
www.inaweek.co.uk